HAPPY WOOL FELT ANIMALS

Happy Wool Felt Animals
First published in the United States in 2020 by Stash Books, an imprint of
C&T Publishing, Inc., P.O. Box 1456, Lafayette, CA 94549

YOMO FERUTO NO HOHOEMU DO BUTSU-TACHI
Copyright ©2014 Makiko Arai/Magazineland.
Original Japanese edition published by Magazineland, Tokyo, Japan
English language rights, translation & production by World Book Media, LLC
Email: info@worldbookmedia.com

Photography: Kohsuke Ugajin and Makiko Arai
Process photography: Akira Takashima
Illustrations: Hiroyuki Oguro
Planning: Toyoko Hirota
Editor: Eriko Ota

English Translation: Mayumi Anzai
English Language Editor: Lindsay Fair
English Edition Layout: Stacy Wakefield Forte

ISBN: 978-1-64403-002-8

Manufactured in China

10 9 8 7 6 5 4 3 2 1

HAPPY WOOL FELT ANIMALS

NEEDLE FELT 30 FURRY & FEATHERED FRIENDS

MAKIKO ARAI

C&T PUBLISHING

INTRODUCTION

The first thing I ever needle felted was a small sheep. I have to admit, that first sheep had a strange shape, but I enjoyed working with wool so much that I haven't been able to stop making needle felt animals ever since.

To me, needle felting with wool is more similar to sculpting with clay than it is to doll-making because you can create any shape you want without following a paper pattern. This is both the most difficult and most rewarding part of working with wool.

If you're new to needle felting, I hope that you're inspired to make your favorite animals without worrying if they look like the examples in this book. Watching these cute creatures come to life out of a fluffy pile of wool will warm your heart!

I've included designs for some of my favorite animals, as well as needle felting basics and some more advanced tips and tricks. It would make me so happy if you find these methods helpful in creating your own needle felted animal friends.

—MAKIKO ARAI

WHITE-EYE BROOCH
Instructions » pages 43 and 81

RABBIT BROOCH
Instructions » page 78

SWAN BROOCH
Instructions » page 72

BROOCH BUDDIES

As small as a flower or a nut, these miniscule brooches feature friends
from the forest and the field. Anyone can make these, even if you've
never needle felted before—just stick wool roving to a piece of felt. Now,
which one of you wants to go out into the world with me today?

DONKEY BROOCH
Instructions » page 76

HEDGEHOG BROOCH
Instructions » page 74

MUSHROOM BROOCH
Instructions » pages 40 and 80

CHIPMUNK BROOCH
Instructions » pages 45 and 81

WHITE-EYE
Instructions » page 84

GREAT TIT
*Instructions »
pages 48 and 82*

**WHITE-TAILED
SPARROW**
Instructions » page 86

A TRIO OF
CHATTY BIRDS

"Spring has finally arrived!"
"Look, I brought you a cherry blossom."
"I'm so happy that it's warm now!"
These colorful birds are chirping away.
Do you ever stop and wonder what they say?

RABBIT
Instructions » pages 52 and 88

A little rabbit stands in a field with his ears aloft and his back straight. He almost looks as if he's about to wave. I wonder if he is seeing me off.

10

A SHY

SQUIRREL

This sweet squirrel found a pretty purple violet. Maybe he's thinking of giving it to someone special.

DONKEY
Instructions » pages 57 and 94

A DONKEY
MARCHING TO THE BEAT
OF HIS OWN DRUM

While out walking, this donkey discovered some leaves with an interesting smell. He's been eyeing them for a while and wondering if they're edible.

HEDGEHOG

A happy hedgehog smells the sweet scent of
a delicious-looking raspberry. Is it ripe yet?

COCKATIEL

Instructions » pages 71 and 102

A COCKATIEL

WITH ROSY CHEEKS

This cockatiel has round red cheeks that look like little
cherries. His hairstyle is pretty cool too, isn't it?

KITTEN

Instructions » pages 62 and 106

A PLAYFUL STRIPED
KITTEN

This adorable kitten may look sweet and docile, but watch out—he's getting ready to pounce on that tempting ball of yarn!

POODLE
*Instructions »
pages 59 and 108*

SHIBA INU
Instructions » page 110

DOGGY FRIENDS

Dogs come in all shapes and sizes. But no matter how different they look, they can become friends very quickly. That's just how dogs are.

SHEEP BROTHERS

Running in the field, play fighting—these sheep brothers are always getting
into trouble together. Now be good until your mom comes back!

A FAMILY OF DEER

IN THE SUMMER

This sweet little fawn is learning how to be a deer from her mama. She feels strong and brave when her mom is around, but still gets a bit lonely when she's left home alone.

POLAR BEARS

"Hey Mom, watch this!" the polar bear cub says to his
mother. She smiles as she listens to him chat away.

BEAR CUBS

WHO WANT TO GROW BIG AND STRONG

"Grrrr!" These bear cubs want to grow up
to be big and strong like their dad.
I think their grrrs need a little more rawrrr.

ELEPHANTS
Instructions » page 124

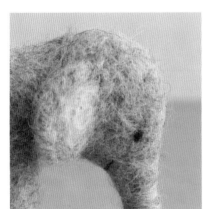

AN ELEPHANT

LEARNING HOW TO USE HER TRUNK

This elephant calf's mother is teaching her how
to use her trunk, but it's harder than it looks. That
delicious-looking fruit is good motivation though.

29

GIRAFFES

IN THE SUN

These serene giraffes are enjoying the sunshine
and warm breeze. Watch them extend their
necks a bit more to reach a tasty leaf.

TOOLS & MATERIALS

WOOL ROVING

A **Merino Wool Roving**
Most of the projects in this book were made with merino or merino blend wool roving. This type of wool roving is known for its soft texture and is available in a wide variety of colors.

B **Natural, Undyed Wool Roving**
This type of wool roving maintains the natural color of the sheep's fleece. Use this wool roving for realistic animal fur coloring with subtle nuances in tone.

C **Core Fiber**
This wool batting works well as a base for larger projects, especially those with a wire frame. It's a fast-felting fiber that is easy to shape.

D **Curly Wool Locks**
Uncombed wool roving locks that are cut from the fleece and washed to remove impurities, and then dried. This type of wool maintains the natural curly texture of the sheep from which it was obtained. Great for replicating fluffy texture, such as poodle fur.

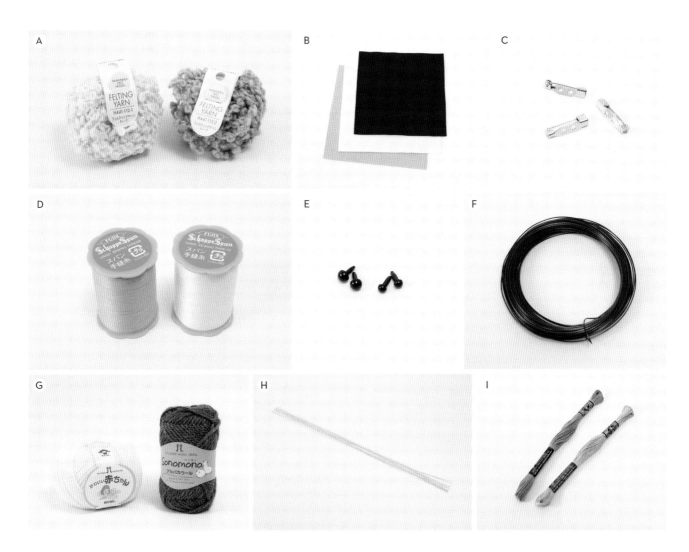

A **Looped Felting Yarn**
100% wool loop yarn that can be felted for a curly, fluffy textured finish. Ideal for replicating sheep fur.

B **Sheet Felt**
Sold in small pieces. Used for the base of brooches and for bird feet. I recommend using wool felt.

C **Brooch Pins**
Sew to the back of a design to transform it into a brooch.

D **Sewing Thread**
Use to sew brooch pins in place.

E **Eye Buttons**
Use 3–4 mm black shank buttons for eyes.

F **Aluminum Craft Wire**
Use 19-gauge (0.9 mm) aluminum craft wire to create bendable figures.

G **Yarn**
Cover wire frames with yarn to create a base for attaching wool roving.

H **Floral Wire**
Use to create the structure for bird legs.

I **Embroidery Floss**
Use to embroider details, such as claws, and to make bird legs.

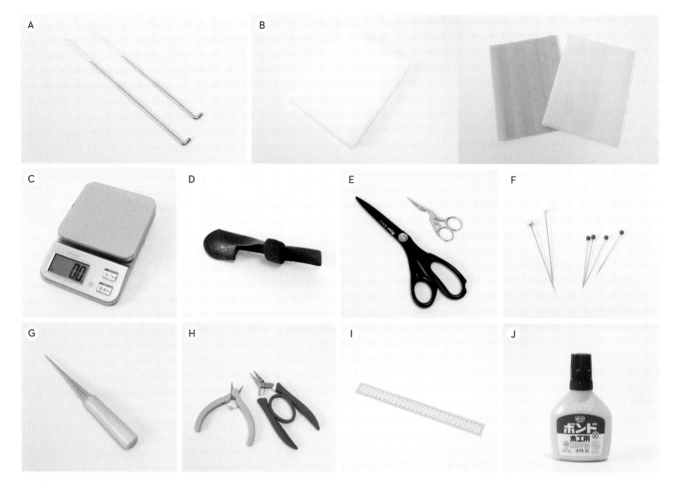

A **Felting Needles**
These special needles feature tiny barbs. When the needle is repeatedly stabbed into the wool roving, the barbs catch the wool fibers, causing them to become tangled. The more the wool roving is felted, the more tangled the fibers become, which makes the piece of felt smaller and denser. Felting needles are available in a variety of sizes. I recommend using a fine gauge needle for the projects in this book.

B **Felting Mat & Mat Covers**
Use a mat underneath your work to protect the felting needle from breaking. Colorful mat covers help you see the color of the wool roving more clearly.

C **Scale**
Use a food scale to weigh out the necessary amount of wool roving. Look for one with an accuracy of 0.5 g or better.

D **Thimble**
Use a leather thimble to protect your fingers from the felting needle.

E **Scissors**
You'll need a large pair of scissors for cutting felt, plus a small pair for cutting thread.

F **Sewing Pins**
Use to temporarily hold body parts in place or to mark the position of facial features.

G **Awl**
Use to create holes for eye buttons.

H **Wire Cutters**
Use to cut metal wire.

I **Ruler**
Use to measure lengths of wool roving and body parts.

J **Craft Glue**
Use to attach eye buttons, bird legs, brooch pins, and other components.

NEEDLE FELTING BASICS

HOW TO SEPARATE A LARGE AMOUNT OF WOOL ROVING

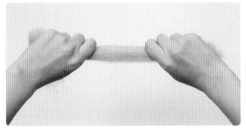 

HOLD THE WOOL roving in two hands, leaving a space about the size of a fist in between. Gently pull to slowly separate the wool roving into two pieces.

HOW TO SEPARATE A SMALL AMOUNT OF WOOL ROVING

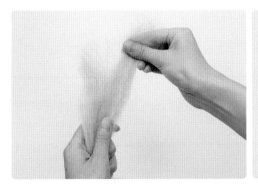 

GRAB A SMALL section from the end of the wool roving and pull slowly.

HOW TO NEEDLE FELT

INSERT THE NEEDLE into the wool roving, then pull it out at the same angle. Be careful not to alter the angle of the needle or force it as this may cause the needle to break. This process of pushing the needle into the wool roving and pulling it out again causes the fibers to tangle and transform into felt.

▶ Oval Shape

  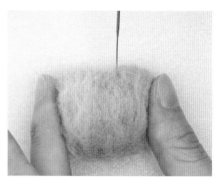

Roll the wool roving into a ball and position it on the mat. Use the felting needle to stab the wool roving in the areas where you want it to become more compact. Roll the wool roving as you go to work all sides evenly. Repeat this process until the wool roving is formed into an oval shape.

▶ Egg Shape

 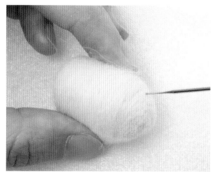 

Use the process described above to make an oval shape. Next, stab one end of the oval to make it pointy, rolling the wool roving as you go to work all sides evenly. If necessary, add more wool roving to the wider end to make it thicker. This technique is used for bird bodies and for the heads of animals with pointed noses.

HOW TO MAKE THE EARS

  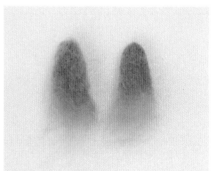

Position a bit of loosened wool roving on the mat. Stab to form the wool roving into a flat, thin shape. Next, hold the work between your fingers and form into shape by stabbing the edges. Wear a thimble or use a piece of thick paper rolled into a tube to protect your finger from the needle. Leave the fibers loose at the base of the ears—this is how they'll be attached to the head.

HOW TO ATTACH BODY PARTS

▶ Use Pins to Attach Temporarily

 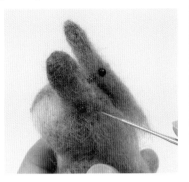  

Large parts, such as the head and body, as well as small parts, such as the ears, arms, legs, and tail, should be temporarily attached using pins. This will allow you to check their placement before permanently attaching with the felting needle.

▶ Permanently Attach by Felting

Stab the loose fibers to attach the body parts. Use scissors to trim excess wool roving, then stab to attach the trimmed fibers.

HOW TO ADD SHADING

  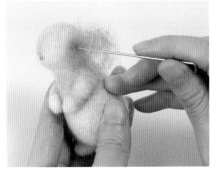

Rub a bit of wool roving between your fingertips to loosen it up until it is nice and fluffy. Position the wool roving on the area of the animal where you'd like to add shading. Use a fine gauge needle to lightly stab the wool roving in place.

Note: This example uses the Rabbit on page 10, but many of the same techniques can be used for other projects in this book.

▶ **Mark the Placement**

Insert pins to mark the position of the eyes and nose. Check to make sure you are happy with the placement before moving on to the next step.

▶ **Make the Nose**

Use the tip of the needle to make three holes marking the nose placement.

Roll a bit of wool roving into a thin rope. Stab the end of the rope into the left hole until it is secure.

Next, stab the rope into the middle hole, and then the right hole to make a V-shape.

Finally, stab the rope back into the left hole (the first hole) to complete the triangle. Trim any excess wool roving.

▶ **Make the Mouth**

Use the tip of the needle to form an indented line marking the mouth placement.

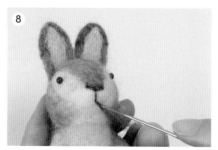

Twist a bit of wool roving into a thin rope.

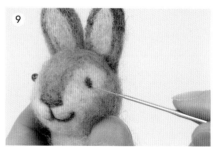

Stab the end of the rope into the line marked in step 6, starting just under the nose. Make sure the end is secure, then continue to fill in along the marked line.

▶ **Make the Eyes**

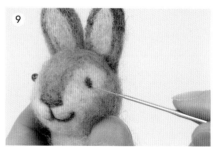

Roll a bit of wool roving into a ball about the size of a sesame seed. Stab to attach each eye at the marked location.

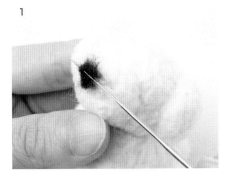

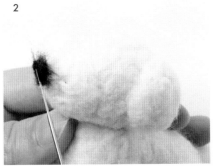

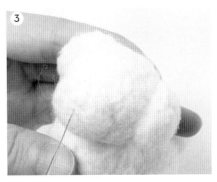

1

If you need to detach a bit of wool roving that has already been felted, insert the tip of the needle into the wool roving that you wish to remove.

2

Pull the wool roving out bit by bit until it is completely removed.

3

Use a fine gauge needle to reshape the area where the wool roving was removed.

The following guide uses the Mushroom Brooch on page 7 as an example, but many of the same techniques apply to the other brooch projects in this book.

tip *Use a fine gauge needle for making brooches as they are small and detailed.*

▶ **Make the Brooch Base**

1

Weigh out the required amount of wool roving.

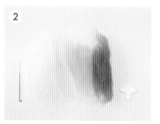

2

Or separate a bit of each color of wool roving. Brooches only require a small amount of wool roving, so there's really no need for exact measurements.

3

Trace the template onto sheet felt, and then cut out the shape. This will be the brooch base.

4

Rub a bit of white wool roving between your fingertips to loosen it up until it is nice and fluffy.

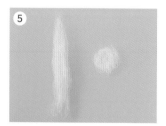

5

The wool roving on the left has just been separated from the bundle, while the wool roving on the right has been loosened and fluffed. This extra step will make it easier to form the wool roving into shape during the felting process.

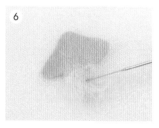

6

Position the loosened wool roving on top of the brooch base cut from felt.

NOTE *Beige felt is used in this example for visual clarity. When making the Mushroom Brooch, use white felt as noted in the materials list on page 80.*

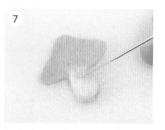

7

Stab the wool roving with the tip of the needle to attach it to the brooch base.

8

Keep adding a bit of wool roving at a time until the entire surface of the brooch is covered. Add a bit more wool roving at the middle of the mushroom to make it plump and give it a three-dimensional shape.

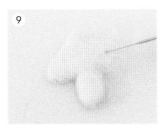

9 Continue felting until the brooch base is completely covered and the surface is smooth.

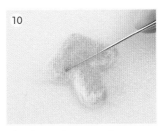

10 Flip the work over and secure any loose wool roving to the felt on the back of the brooch. Make sure that the felt is completely covered along the edges of the brooch.

11 Hold the mushroom stem between your fingers and form into shape by stabbing the edges. Make sure to wear a thimble to protect your finger.

12 If you don't have a thimble, you can make one by rolling some thick paper into a tube.

▶ Felt the Mushroom Cap

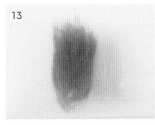

13 You'll need to mix red and orange wool roving in a 2:1 ratio. Start by aligning the two colors of wool roving side by side.

14 Hold the wool roving in two hands and gently pull to separate a bit of each color. Realign the separated pieces on top of the rest of the bundle.

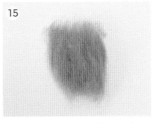

15 Continue breaking the wool roving apart and realigning it until the colors are thoroughly mixed.

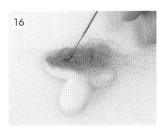

16 Stab the mixed red orange wool roving onto the mushroom cap. Form it into shape so it is a bit more plump in the middle.

▶ Felt the Stem

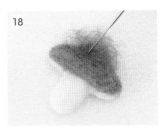

17 Secure any loose wool roving to the felt on the back of the brooch and form the cap into shape along the edges (refer to steps 10–12 above).

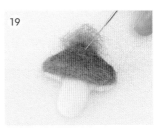

18 Cover the middle and tip of the cap with a thin layer of red wool roving.

19 Cover the tip of the cap with another thin layer of red wool roving to create a gradated effect.

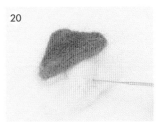

20 Cover the bottom of the stem with a bit of beige wool roving and stab it in place, wrapping it around the bottom.

▶ Embellish the Cap

21

This technique will give the bottom of the stem a nice round shape.

22

Roll a tiny bit of white wool roving between your fingertips to make a ball.

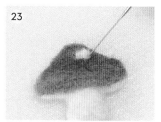

23

Stab the ball in place on the mushroom cap.

24

Repeat the process to make various sizes of wool roving balls and stab them in place on the mushroom cap.

▶ Attach a Brooch Pin

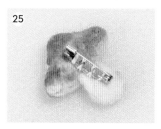

25

Sew a brooch pin to the felt on the back of the brooch. Take care that the stitches are not visible on the front of the brooch.

26

Alternatively, you can sew a brooch pin to a scrap of sheet felt, then trim it into shape and glue it to the back of the brooch.

HOW TO CREATE SHADING WITH WOOL ROVING

The following guide uses the White-Eye Brooch on page 6 as an example, but many of the same techniques apply to the other projects in this book.

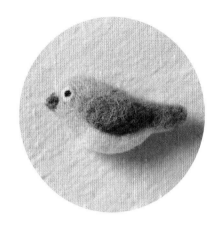

tip *Use a fine gauge needle for making brooches as they are small and detailed.*

▶ Make the Brooch Base

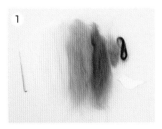

Separate a bit of each color of wool roving. Trace the template onto sheet felt and cut out the shape to make the brooch base.

Stab the white wool roving onto the brooch base, adding a bit more wool roving at the middle to make the wings plump.

NOTE *Beige felt is used in this example for visual clarity. When making the White-Eye Brooch, use white felt as noted in the materials list on page 81.*

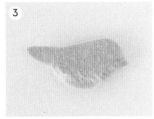

Flip the work over and secure any loose wool roving to the felt on the back of the brooch, making sure that the felt is completely covered along the edges of the brooch. Hold the work between your fingers and form into shape by stabbing the edges (refer to steps 10–12 on page 41).

▶ Felt the Head & Back

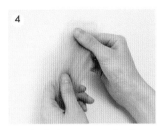

Mix the light green and yellow wool roving in a 1:1 ratio (refer to step 14 on page 41).

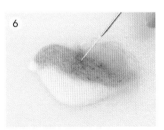

Stab the mixed wool roving made in step 4 onto the head and back of the bird. Secure any loose wool roving to the felt on the back of the brooch and form into shape by stabbing the edges.

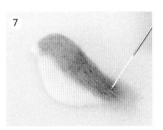

Cover half of the back and the tail with a thin layer of light green wool roving.

Cover the tail with another thin layer of light green wool roving to create a gradated effect.

▶ Felt the Wing & Tail

Mix the light green and dark green wool roving in a 2:1 ratio.

9

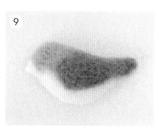

Stab the mixed wool roving made in step 8 onto the wing and tip of the tail.

10

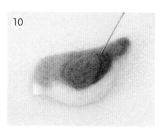

Stab a bit of dark green wool roving onto the tip of the wing.

▶ Felt the Chest

11

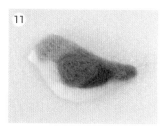

Stab a bit of yellow wool roving onto the chest.

▶ Felt the Beak

12

Stab a bit of brown wool roving onto the beak.

13

Use the tip of the needle to form an indented line, dividing the beak in two.

▶ Felt the Eye

14

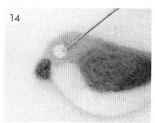

Stab a bit of white wool roving onto the head to create a circle shape for the eye.

15

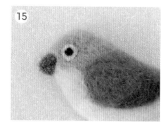

Roll a bit of black wool roving between your fingertips to make an eye about the size of a sesame seed. Stab in place at the center of the white circle.

▶ Attach a Brooch Pin

16

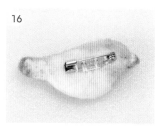

Sew a brooch pin to the felt on the back of the brooch as shown in steps 25–26 on page 42.

HOW TO CREATE A THREE-DIMENSIONAL SHAPE

The following guide uses the Chipmunk Brooch on page 7 as an example, but many of the same techniques apply to the other projects in this book.

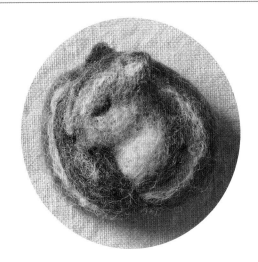

tip *Use a fine gauge needle for making brooches as they are small and detailed.*

▶ Make the Brooch Base

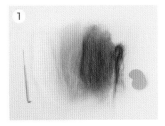

1

Separate a bit of each color of wool roving. Trace the template onto sheet felt and cut out the shape to make the brooch base.

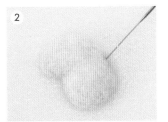

2

Stab the white wool roving onto the brooch base, adding a bit more wool roving at the middle of the chipmunk to make it plump. The white wool roving along the chest and lower half of the face will be visible on the finished brooch, so make sure you're satisfied with how it looks before moving on to the next step.

3

Stab a bit of loosened light brown wool roving onto the brooch base on the upper half of the head and along the back and bottom of the chipmunk.

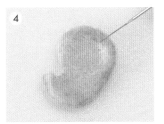

4

Flip the work over and secure any loose wool roving to the felt on the back of the brooch, making sure that the felt is completely covered along the edges of the brooch. Hold the work between your fingers and form into shape by stabbing along the edges (refer to steps 10–12 on page 41).

▶ Make the Ears

5

Rub a bit of brown wool roving between your fingertips to loosen it up until it is nice and fluffy.

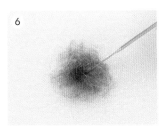

6

Position the loosened wool roving on top of the mat and stab it at the center to begin felting it into shape.

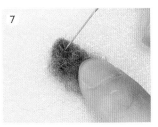

7

Fold the top edges in toward the center to form the wool roving into the shape of an ear. Flip the work over and follow the same process on the back.

8

Hold the work between your fingers and form into shape by stabbing the edges. Use a thimble or piece of thick paper to protect your index finger.

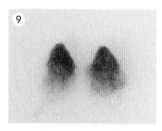

9

Leave the wool roving fibers loose at the base of the ear. Repeat steps 5–9 to make a second ear.

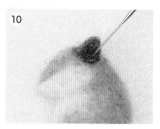

10

Stab the loose fibers to attach one ear to the head.

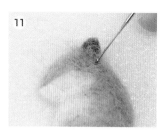

11

Stab a bit of loosened light brown wool roving to the head at the base of the ear and inside the ear, leaving the outer edges brown.

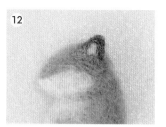

12

Stab a bit of white wool roving inside the ear.

▶ Make the Stripes

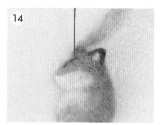

13

Stab the loose fibers to attach the other ear to the head on the back of the brooch.

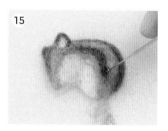

14

Take a thin strip of brown wool roving and start attaching it to the center of the face, starting just above the nose.

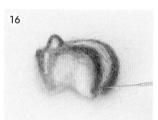

15

Continue attaching the stripe down the center of the back, and then attach another brown stripe (refer to the Color Key on page 81 and the photo on page 7 for placement).

16

Use the same process to attach the white stripes.

▶ Felt the Nose & Eye

17

Roll a bit of dark brown wool roving between your fingertips to make a ball about the size of a sesame seed. Stab it in place on the tip of the chipmunk's nose.

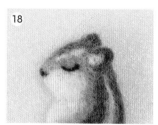

18

Stab small holes to mark the ends of the eye (refer to the Color Key on page 81 for placement). Roll a thin strip of dark brown wool roving between your fingertips to make a rope, then stab it in place to make the eye.

▶ Make the Tail

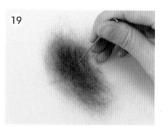

19

Loosen a bit of brown wool roving and arrange into the shape of a fairly large tail. Begin felting into shape, leaving the fibers loose at the base of the tail.

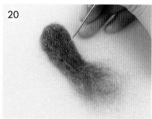

20

Once the general shape of the tail is formed, add some fluffy brown wool roving to give the tail a bushy texture.

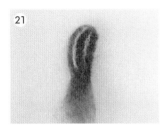

21

Stab thin strips of white wool roving to the tail to create stripes.

22

Use a pin to temporarily attach the loose fibers at the base of the tail to the back of the brooch. Fold the tail around to the front to check placement and length.

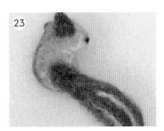

23

Stab the loose fibers at the base of the tail to the back of the brooch to secure the tail in place.

24

Tuck the tip of the tail behind the chipmunk's head and secure in place by stabbing it to the back of the brooch.

▶ **Attach a Brooch Pin**

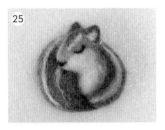

25

Adjust the shape of the tail so it wraps around the chipmunk's body.

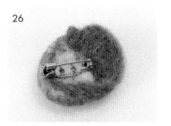

26

Sew a brooch pin to the felt on the back of the brooch as shown in steps 25–26 on page 42.

The following guide uses the Great Tit on page 9 as an example, but many of the same techniques apply to the other projects in this book.

tip *I prefer to work with a fine gauge needle, but you may want to use a regular needle for attaching the head and body more quickly.*

▶ Make the Head

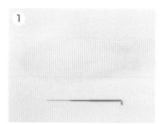

Separate a bit of white wool roving to make the head.

Roll it into a ball using the template on page 83 as a guide.

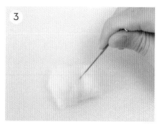

Stab the top surface to begin forming into shape.

Continue stabbing on all sides, rolling into a tight ball as you work. Gradually add a bit more wool roving to increase the size if necessary.

▶ Make the Body

The ball will become smaller and more compact as you felt it. Flatten the ball slightly as indicated by the side view template on page 83.

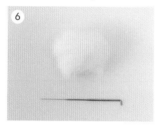

To make the body, separate a bit more white wool roving than was used to make the head. Roll it into an oval using the template on page 83 as a guide.

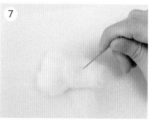

Stab the top surface to begin forming the body into shape.

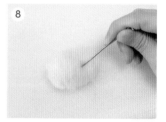

Continue stabbing on all sides, rolling into a tight oval as you work. Gradually add a bit more wool roving to increase the size if necessary.

▶ Attach the Head to the Body

Gradually add a bit more wool roving to transform the oval into a flattened egg shape, as indicated by the side view template on page 83.

Use a pin to temporarily attach the head to the body.

Begin stabbing along the area where the head connects to the body to create the neck. Stab from the body toward the head.

Next, stab from the head toward the body until the two pieces are completely attached.

▶ Smooth Out the Neck

13

Completed view once the head is attached to the body.

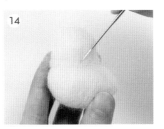

14

Add a bit of loosened wool roving to the neck.

15

Add a bit more loosened wool roving to the areas of the neck you'd like to build up, then stab to form into shape.

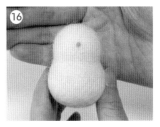

16

Insert a pin to mark the placement of the beak. Add a bit of loosened white wool roving to both sides of the face to make the cheeks more plump.

▶ Add Color to the Head

17

Position some loosened black wool roving on top of the head and begin stabbing it into place.

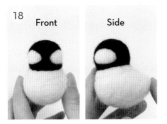

18 Front   Side

Make the entire head black, leaving the areas around the eyes and cheeks uncovered.

▶ Make the Tail

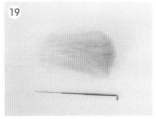

19

Separate a bit of gray wool roving. Fold it in half and position it on top of the mat.

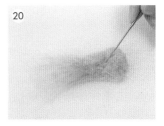

20

Stab the wool roving to begin forming it into the shape of a tail. Flip the work over and follow the same process on the back.

21

Hold the work between your fingers and form into shape by stabbing the edges.

22 Before   After

The wool roving will become smaller and more compact as it takes shape.

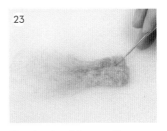

23

Use the tip of the needle to form indented lines on the tail.

24

Use pins to attach the tail to the body. Stab the loosened fibers at the base of the tail to attach it to the bird.

25

Add a bit of white wool roving underneath the base of the tail to add a little support.

26

Under   Side

Completed view once the white wool roving has been added under the tail.

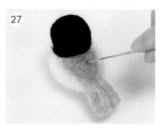

27

Stab a bit of loosened sage green wool roving from the neck down to the base of the tail.

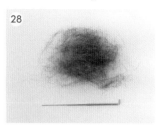

28

Separate a bit of dark gray wool roving to make a wing.

29

Position the wool roving on top of the mat and stab it at the center to begin forming it into a wing shape.

30

Stab the edges to form the wool roving into a triangular wing shape.

31

Use your fingers to hold the wing in place on the mat as you continue to form it into shape. Leave the fibers loose at the base of the wing.

32

Repeat steps 28–31 to make another wing. Use pins to attach the wings to the body, then stab to secure in place.

▶ **Add Color to the Wings**

33

Continue stabbing the loose fibers to form them into the shape of a wing.

34

Completed view once the wings have been attached.

35

Stab a bit of loosened gray wool roving to the wings, leaving the tips uncovered.

36

Stab a bit of loosened sage green wool roving on top, leaving about half of each wing uncovered.

▶ Finish the Chest & Belly

37

Add a line of white wool roving to the center of each wing.

38

Completed view of the wing.

39

Add a light layer of loosened white wool roving to the chest and belly. This will give the bird a puffy shape and fluffy texture.

40

Add a black line to the chest.

▶ Make the Beak

41

Separate a bit of dark gray wool roving and roll it into a small ball. Stab to attach the beak to the face at the position marked in step 16.

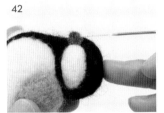

42

Form the beak into shape by stabbing the tip. Add a bit more dark gray wool if necessary.

43

Rub a bit of white wool roving between your fingers to form it into a thin rope. Stab it in place to divide the beak in two.

▶ Attach the Eyes

44

Insert pins to mark the position of the eyes.

45

Use an awl to make holes at the marked locations.

46

Insert the eye buttons and glue them in place.

▶ Make the Feet

47

Use the template on page 83 to cut the feet out of dark brown sheet felt.

48

Glue the feet to the bottom of the bird.

The following guide uses the Rabbit on page 10 as an example, but many of the same techniques apply to the other projects in this book.

▶ Make the Head

▶ Make the Body

Form white wool roving into an egg shape using the template on page 89 as a guide (also refer to page 36).

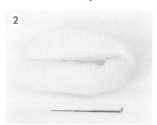

Measure out the amount of wool roving required to make the body. Fold it in half.

Wrap tightly with more wool roving and stab.

Stab, rolling the wool roving as you go to work all sides evenly and form an elongated oval shape. Add more wool roving if necessary.

Continue until the body matches the shape of the template on page 89. Leave the fibers loose at one end.

Trim the excess wool roving to create a nice flat edge.

▶ Attach the Head to the Body

Use a pin to temporarily attach the head to the body.

Begin stabbing along the area where the head connects to the body. This will create the neck. Stab from the body toward the head.

Next, stab from the head toward the body until the two pieces are completely attached.

▶ Smooth Out the Neck

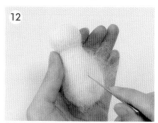

Remove the pin. Add a bit of loosened white wool roving to the neck.

Add a bit more loosened white wool roving to the areas of the neck you'd like to build up, then stab to form into shape.

▶ Make the Body Rounder

Add a bit of loosened white wool roving to the back.

13

Stab to give the body a nice round shape.

14

Insert a pin to mark the placement of the nose. Add a bit of loosened white wool roving to the cheeks and haunches to make them more plump.

▶ Add Color to the Head & Body

15
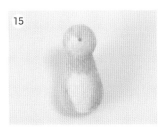

Loosen up a bit of light brown wool roving and stab it to the head and body, leaving the areas around the mouth and belly uncovered.

16
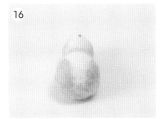

Don't forget to add some to the bottom as well.

▶ Make the Arms

17
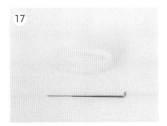

Separate a bit of white wool roving and fold it in half.

18
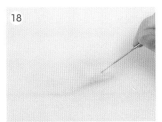

Wrap with a bit more white wool roving and stab, rolling as you go to work all sides evenly.

19

Continue until the arm matches the shape of the template on page 89. Leave the fibers loose at one end. Repeat steps 17–19 to make another arm.

20
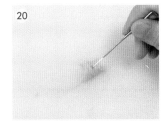

Wrap a thin layer of light brown wool roving around each arm, leaving the paw uncovered. Stab in place to secure.

▶ Make the Legs

21
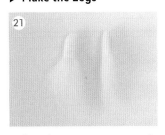

Follow the same process used in steps 17–19 to make two legs, but make them flatter than the arms. Use the template on page 89 as a guide.

▶ Attach the Arms & Legs

22
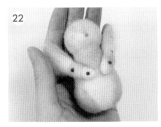

Use pins to temporarily attach the arms to the body.

23

Stab the loose fibers to secure in place. Trim the excess wool roving.

24

Add a bit of light brown wool roving to the areas where the arms attach to the body. Stab to secure and form into shape.

▶ Add Color to the Body

25

Use pins to temporarily attach the legs to the body. Stab the loose fibers to secure in place. Trim the excess wool roving.

26

Add a bit more white wool roving to the areas where the legs attach to the body. Stab to secure and form into shape.

27

Rub a bit of brown wool roving between your fingertips to loosen it up until it is nice and fluffy.

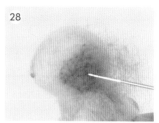

28

Attach the brown wool roving to the head just inside the areas of light brown wool roving.

29

Front view once the brown wool roving has been added to the head.

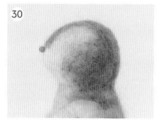

30

Side view once the brown wool roving has been added to the head.

31

Add a bit of loosened brown wool roving to the neck, shoulders, and areas where the arms connect to the body.

32

Add a bit of loosened brown wool roving to the back and bottom.

▶ Make the Tail

33

Add a bit more loosened brown wool roving to the arms, leaving the paws uncovered.

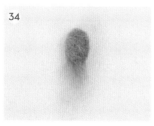

34

Follow the same process used in steps 17–19 to make the tail out of brown wool roving (use the template on page 89 as a guide).

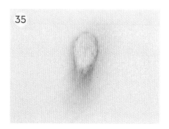

35

Add a bit of loosened white wool roving to the bottom of the tail.

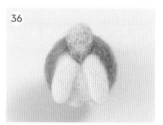

36

Use a pin to temporarily attach the tail to the bottom of the rabbit, then stab to secure in place.

▶ Make the Ears

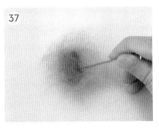

37

Position some loosened brown wool roving on top of the mat and stab it at the center to begin felting into shape.

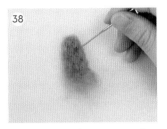

38

Fold the top edges in toward the center to form it into the shape of an ear. Flip the work over and follow the same process on the back.

39

Hold the work between your fingers and form into shape by stabbing the edges. Use a thimble or piece of thick paper to protect your index finger.

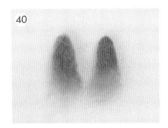

40

Make two ears using the template on page 89 as a guide. Leave the fibers loose at the base of the ears.

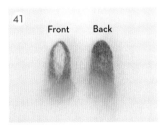

41 Front   Back

Loosen up a bit of dark brown wool roving and stab it to the tips of the ears. Next, stab some white wool roving inside the ears.

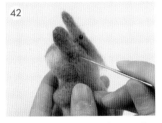

42

Use pins to temporarily attach the ears to the head. Stab the loose fibers to permanently attach the ears to the back of the head. Trim the excess if necessary.

▶ Felt the Nose & Mouth

43

Insert pins to mark the placement of the eyes and nose (refer to page 38).

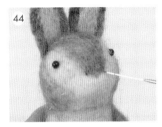

44

Use the tip of the needle to make holes marking the nose placement.

45

Roll a bit of dark brown wool roving into a thin rope. Stab the rope into the holes to make a triangular nose, then trim the excess.

46

Use the tip of the needle to form an indented line marking the mouth placement. Attach a thin rope of dark brown wool roving following the marked line.

▶ Felt the Eyes

47

Roll bits of dark brown wool roving into balls about the size of sesame seeds and stab to attach the eyes at the marked locations.

48

Completed view after all the facial features have been added.

The following guide uses the Squirrel on page 11 as an example, but many of the same techniques apply to the other projects in this book.

▶ **Make the Tail**	▶ **Add More Wool Roving to the Tail**

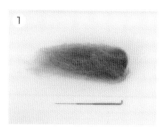

Separate a bit of brown wool roving and fold it in half so it measures about 3 in (8 cm) in length.

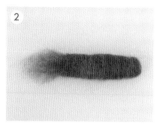

Wrap with a bit more brown wool roving and stab, rolling as you go to work all sides evenly. Continue until the tail matches the size and shape of the template on page 91.

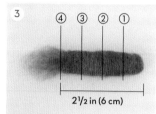

Next, you'll add a bit more brown wool roving to the tail four times, about every ⅝ in (1.5 cm). This will make the tail thicker along the 2½ in (6 cm) section.

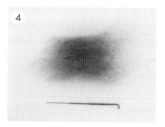

Start by positioning a bit of brown wool roving on top of the mat to make a thin layer about 2½ in (6 cm) long and 1½ in (4 cm) wide.

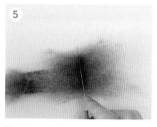

Position the bundle of wool roving from step 4 on top of the tip of the tail, so the center aligns with line ①.

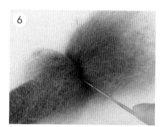

Stab along the center of the bundle to attach it to the tip of the tail.

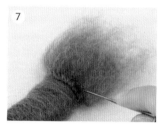

Fold the bundled wool toward the tip of the tail. Stab about ¼ in (5 mm) from the fold to secure in place.

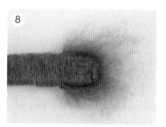

Flip the work over and add some more wool roving to the back following the same process used in steps 4–7.

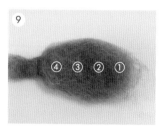

Add some more brown wool roving to the front and back of the tail three more times following the process used in steps 4–8. Use scissors to trim the excess wool roving into shape according to the template on page 91.

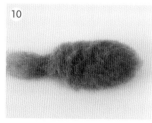

Completed view after trimming the extra wool roving.

Use pins to temporarily attach the base of the tail to the bottom of the squirrel. Stab to secure in place.

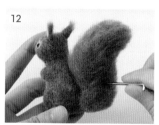

Secure the rest of the tail to the body in a few spots by stabbing the needle deeply from the back side of the tail. Shape the tail with your hands.

The following guide uses the Donkey on page 12 as an example, but many of the same techniques apply to the other projects in this book.

▶ Make the Head

1

Separate about 1 g of white wool roving. Tie a knot at the center and fold it in half.

2

Wrap another 1 g of white wool roving around it to shape the head, with the knot serving as the nose. Stab, rolling the wool roving as you go to work all sides evenly and shape according to the template on page 97.

3

Wrap a bit of brown wool roving around the head, leaving the tip of the nose uncovered.

▶ Make the Body

4

Separate an 8 in (20 cm) long piece of brown wool roving and fold it in half. Wrap with a bit more brown wool roving and stab to start shaping the body.

5

Follow the same process used in steps 2–5 on page 52 to make the donkey's body.

6

To make the neck, wrap a bit of brown wool roving around the loose fibers at the base of the body. Stab while holding the neck at an upward angle using your left hand.

▶ Attach the Head to the Body

7

Attach the head to the body following the same process used in steps 7–11 on page 52. Next, smooth out the neck area.

▶ Make the Legs

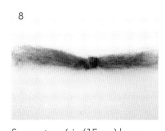

8

Separate a 6 in (15 cm) long piece of dark gray wool roving. Tie a knot in the center. The knot will serve as the hoof.

9

Fold in half. Wrap a bit of brown wool roving around the leg, leaving the hoof uncovered. Stab to secure in place.

10

Stab, rolling the wool roving as you go to work all sides evenly. Make sure the fibers are tightly felted so the leg will be able to support the body.

11

Wrap a bit of white wool roving around the leg, just above the hoof and stab in place. Repeat steps 8–11 to make a total of four legs.

12

Use pins to temporarily attach the legs to the body. If necessary, adjust the position of the legs so that the donkey stands up by itself.

13

Stab to permanently attach the loose fibers at the base of each leg to the body.

14

Add some loosened brown wool roving to the areas where the legs connect to the body.

15

Completed view after stabbing more wool roving to the legs.

16

Next, add a bit more wool roving to the top of the legs to make the thighs fuller.

The following guide uses the Poodle on page 18 as an example, but many of the same techniques apply to the other projects in this book.

▶ Make the Head

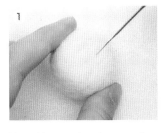

1

Use white wool roving to make the head, following the process used in steps 1–5 on page 48.

2

Stab the bottom of the circle to make the area where the head attaches to the body flat, using the template on page 109 as a guide.

3

Loosen the curly wool locks by rubbing a bit between your fingertips.

▶ Add the Fur to the Head

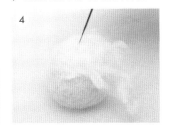

4

Stab to attach the curly wool locks to the head.

▶ Add the Snout & Ears

5

Cover the head with the curly wool locks, except for the flat bottom where the head will attach to the body.

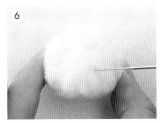

6

Make the snout by stabbing a bit of the curly wool locks to the head, slightly beneath the center.

7

View from the side after adding the snout. Make sure that the fibers are densely felted so you'll be able to add the facial features later.

8

Position a bit of the curly wool locks on the mat and felt into the shape of a round ear. Repeat the process to make a second ear.

9

Stab to attach the ears to the side of the head. Stab around the ear, leaving a bit of the fluffy texture.

10

View from the top after attaching the ears. Make sure to attach the ears not just on the side, but slightly toward the back of the head.

▶ Make the Body

11

Use white wool roving to make the body, following the process used in steps 6–8 on page 48.

12

Form the body into a curved shape, using the template on page 109 as a guide.

▶ Attach the Head to the Body

13

Attach the head to the body, following the process used in steps 10–13 on pages 48–49.

▶ Make the Front Legs

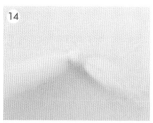

14

Separate a 6 in (15 cm) long piece of white wool roving. Tie a knot in the center. The knot will serve as the paw.

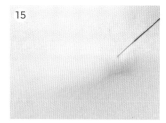

15

Fold in half. Wrap a bit of white wool roving around the leg. Stab to secure in place and shape the leg.

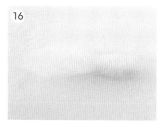

16

Make two front legs, using the template on page 109 as a guide. Leave the fibers loose at the base of each leg.

▶ Attach the Front Legs to the Body

17

Stab some curly wool locks to the paws.

18

Use pins to temporarily attach the front legs to the body. Check the placement from both the front and side to make sure it looks like the dog is sitting.

19

Once you are happy with the placement, stab the loose fibers to secure the front legs to the body.

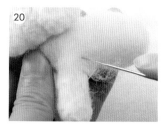

20

If an indentation forms while attaching the legs to the body, add a bit more loosened wool roving to the body.

▶ Add Fur to the Body

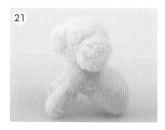

21

Check the stability of the legs by positioning the work on a flat surface.

22

Attach the curly wool locks to the entire body and the front legs.

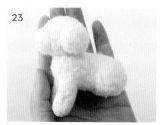

23

Add a bit more curly wool locks to the back to make the haunches more plump.

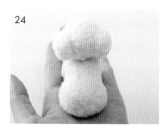

24

View after adding some more curly wool locks to the haunches. The bottom looks round when viewed from the back.

▶ Make the Back Legs

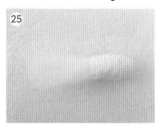
25

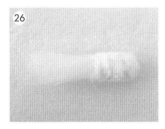
26

27

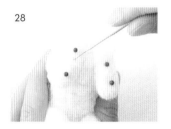
28

Make two back legs, following the same process used for the front legs. Use the template on page 109 as a guide.

Add some curly wool locks.

Use pins to temporarily attach the back legs right under the haunches.

Stab the loose fibers to attach the back legs to the body. Trim the excess wool roving and stab the loose fibers in place.

▶ Make the Tail

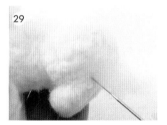
29

30

31

32

If an indentation forms while attaching the legs to the body, add a bit more loosened wool roving to the body.

View after attaching the back legs.

Roll some curly wool locks into a ball, then stab to felt into a round tail shape. Flatten the part where the tail will attach to the body.

Use pins to temporarily attach the tail to the body. Stab to attach the tail.

▶ Felt the Nose, Eyes & Mouth

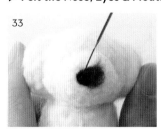
33

34

▶ Add a Bow

35

Roll a bit of dark brown wool roving into a ball. Stab to attach the nose to the snout.

Follow the process used on page 38 to make the eyes and mouth out of dark brown wool roving.

Tie a ribbon around the neck to make a bow.

The following guide uses the Kitten on page 16 as an example, but many of the same techniques apply to the other projects in this book.

▶ Make the Head

1

Use white wool roving to make an egg-shaped head, as shown on page 36.

▶ Make the Body

2

You'll make the chest and back separately. First, fold a bit of white wool roving into shape using the back template on page 107. Wrap a bit more white wool roving around it.

3

Stab the top surface to form the body into a curved egg shape.

4

Once the top surface is densely felted and has a nice round shape, flip the work over and stab the bottom surface which was facing the mat earlier and flatten it.

5

Completed view of the back. It should have an egg shape when viewed from above.

6

Follow the same process to make the chest.

7

Use pins to temporarily attach the chest and back. Stab from both directions to attach the two pieces.

▶ Smooth Out the Shape

8

Wrap a bit of loosened white wool roving around the area where the chest and back connect. Stab to secure, smoothing out the shape.

▶ Attach the Head to the Body

9

Use a pin to temporarily attach the head to the body. Stab from the body toward the head. Next, stab from the head toward the body until the two pieces are completely attached. This will create the neck.

▶ Smooth Out the Neck

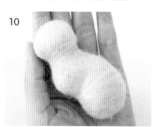

10

Remove the pin. Add a bit of loosened wool roving to the neck and stab to smooth out the shape.

▶ Make the Front Legs

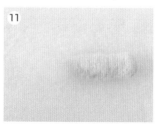

11

Use white wool roving to make two front legs, following the process used in steps 14–16 on page 60.

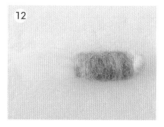

12

Wrap a bit of gray wool roving around each leg, leaving the paws uncovered.

▶ Embroider the Claws

13

Thread the embroidery floss onto a needle, fold in half, and tie a knot at the end. You'll use this thread to embroider three claws onto each paw.

14

Insert the needle through the paw from the back side of the leg (the side that will be attached to the body). Draw the needle out at the starting position of the first claw.

15

Pull the needle and thread taut so that the knot becomes hidden inside the wool roving.

16

Insert the needle back through the paw at the ending position of the first claw, and then draw it out at the starting position of the second claw.

17

Insert the needle back through the paw at the ending position of the second claw, and then draw it out at the starting position of the third claw.

18

Insert the needle back through the paw at the ending position of the third claw, and then draw it out from the spot where you hid the knot in step 15.

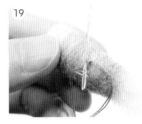

19

Make a knot, and then insert the needle back through the leg in a different direction to hide the knot inside the wool roving, pull the thread taut, and trim the excess thread.

20

Completed view after embroidering three claws onto the paw. Repeat for the other leg.

▶ Attach the Front Legs to the Body

21

Use pins to temporarily attach the front legs to the body, then stab the loose fibers to secure.

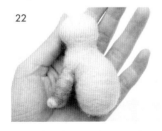

22

Completed view after attaching the front legs.

▶ Build Up the Haunches

23

Add some loosened white wool roving to the haunches to make them more plump at the sides.

▶ Make the Back Legs

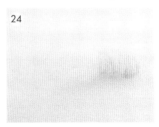

24

Make two back legs, following the process used in steps 14–16 on page 60. Use the template on page 107 as a guide.

25

Follow the same process used in steps 13–20 on page 63 to embroider three claws on each paw.

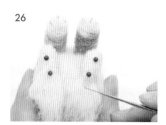

26

Use pins to temporarily attach the back legs right under the haunches. Stab the loose fibers to attach the back legs to the body.

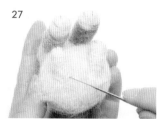

27

Trim the excess wool roving and stab the loose fibers in place. If necessary, add a bit more loosened wool roving to the areas where the legs connect to the body and stab to smooth out the shape.

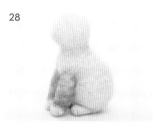

28

Completed view after attaching the back legs.

▶ Make the Ears

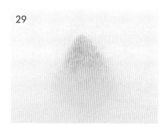

29

Use light brown wool roving to make two triangular ears, as shown on page 36.

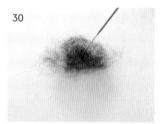

30

Loosen a bit of dark gray wool roving and stab it on the back of each ear. Stab it lightly so that it doesn't come out on the other side.

31

Flip each ear over and stab some more dark gray wool roving along the edges.

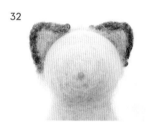

32

Insert a pin to mark the nose placement. Use pins to temporarily attach the ears to the head, bending them slightly.

▶ Add Color to the Body

33

View from the side after attaching the ears with pins.

34

Stab the loose fibers to attach the ears to the head. Trim the excess wool roving and stab the loose fibers in place.

35

Stab a bit of loosened light brown wool roving onto the chest.

36

Stab a bit more light brown wool roving from the belly to the haunches.

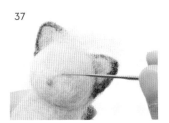

37

Stab a bit of loosened light brown wool roving starting from the nose and continuing to the top of the head.

38

Stab a bit of loosened light brown wool roving onto the cheeks and all around the head. Leave the areas around the eyes and mouth white.

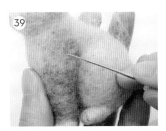

39

Stab a bit of loosened gray wool roving to the body, starting at the areas where the front legs connect to the body and continuing across the shoulders.

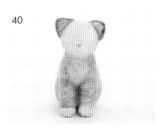

40

View from the front after stabbing some gray wool roving onto the shoulders.

▶ **Add the Facial Features**

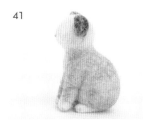

41

Stab a bit of loosened gray wool roving to the back and the bottom.

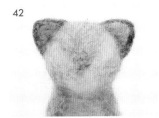

42

Stab a bit of loosened gray wool roving to the nose, cheeks, and all around the head.

43

Stab a bit of gray wool roving to the back of the head.

44

Use dark gray wool roving to make the nose and black wool roving to make the eyes and mouth, as shown on page 38.

▶ **Add the Stripes to the Body**

45

Separate a thin strip of dark gray wool roving. Stab it in place on one of the front legs.

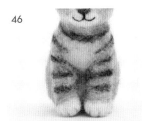

46

Make three horizontal stripes on each front leg. Continue the striped pattern on the neck and shoulders, using the photo on page 16 as a reference.

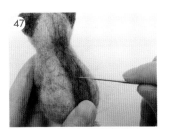

47

Stab a thick vertical stripe of dark gray wool roving to the back, starting at the neck and continuing all the way to the bottom.

48

Add horizontal stripes to the back, aligning the stripes with those on the front legs and shoulders.

▶ Add Some Stripes to the Face

▶ Make the Tail

49

Add a few thin vertical stripes to the back of the head.

50

Add a few thin vertical stripes to the forehead, then add a few thin diagonal stripes to the cheeks.

51

View from the side after adding stripes to the face.

52

Separate a bit of dark gray wool roving and fold it to size using the template on page 107. Wrap with a bit more dark gray wool roving, then stab into shape.

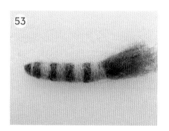

53

Wrap a thin layer of gray wool roving around the tail and stab in place. Next, add stripes using dark gray wool roving.

54

Use pins to temporarily attach the tail to the bottom. Stab to attach the loose fibers at the base of the tail to the body.

55

Wrap the tail around the curve of the bottom, then stab to secure the tip of the tail to the back leg.

The following guide uses the Sheep on page 20 as an example, but many of the same techniques apply to the other projects in this book.

▶ **Make the Wire Frame**

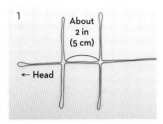

Cut a 24–28 in (60–70 cm) long piece of wire. Fold it in half, then bend it into shape as shown above.

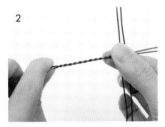

Twist the two pieces of wire together. Start twisting at the head, then continue with the front legs, torso, back legs, and tail.

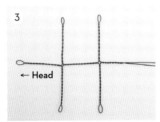

The length of the head and limbs should be around 2–2½ in (5–6 cm).

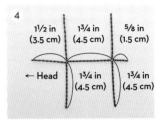

Trim the excess wire so that the frame matches the dimensions listed above.

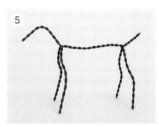

Bend the wire frame into the shape of a sheep's body.

Cut a 8 in (20 cm) long piece of wire. Wrap it around the head, neck, and back. Finish the end by wrapping it around the base of one of the back legs.

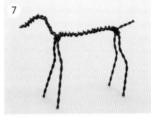

Completed view after wrapping the wire along the head, neck, and back.

▶ **Wrap Yarn Around the Frame**

Tie a piece of yarn around the neck, and then wrap it around the wire frame.

▶ **Add Wool Roving**

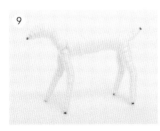

Completed view after wrapping the yarn around the wire frame. This will serve as a base for attaching wool roving.

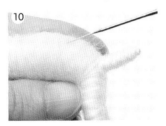

Wrap some white wool roving around the frame and stab it in place. Make sure to insert the needle at an angle when stabbing.

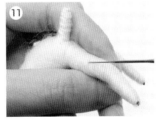

It's important to hold the needle at an angle, otherwise, the needle may break when it hits the wire.

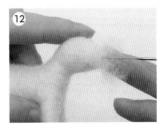

Add some loosened white wool roving to the head and stab to form into shape.

▶ Make the Hooves

13

Completed view after adding white wool roving to the head, body, legs, and tail.

14

Position a bit of loosened light brown wool roving on the mat and begin stabbing into shape.

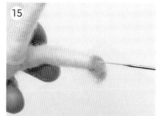

15

Stab to attach the light brown wool roving to one of the feet. Repeat for each of the hooves.

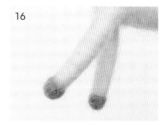

16

Completed view of the hooves.

▶ Make the Body More Round

▶ Make the Fleece

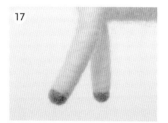

17

Make the legs thicker by wrapping with white wool roving and stabbing in place.

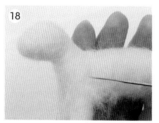

18

Add some more wool roving to the bottom and the shoulders to give the body a more rounded shape.

19

Wrap the felting yarn around the face and stab to secure. Try to insert the needle shallowly and at an angle. Leave the nose uncovered.

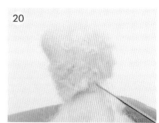

20

Continue wrapping the felting yarn without leaving any gaps and stab it firmly in place.

▶ Make the Ears

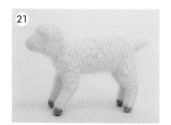

21

Stab felting yarn to the body, tail, and legs, stopping at the knees.

22

Use white wool roving to make two ears, as shown on page 36. Add a bit of pink wool roving to the inside.

23

Trim the loose fibers at the base of the ears with scissors.

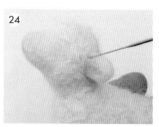

24

Stab the base of the ears firmly to attach to the sheep's head.

▶ Add the Facial Features

25

The ears should form a straight line when viewed from above.

26

Stab some loosened pink wool roving around the nose.

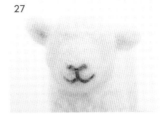

27

Use brown wool roving to make the nose and mouth, as shown on page 38.

28

Roll bits of black wool roving into balls about the size of sesame seeds and stab in place at the position to attach the eyes.

Using a wire frame allows you to change the animals' poses and incorporate movement into your designs. These playful sheep bounce, run, and jump!

The following guide uses the Bears on page 26 as an example, but many of the same techniques apply to the other projects in this book.

▶ Make the Wire Frame

Make a wire frame following the dimensions listed in the individual project instructions. Also refer to steps 1–7 on page 67.

▶ Wrap Yarn Around the Frame

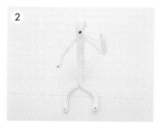

Wrap the yarn around the wire frame to make it thicker, as shown in step 8 on page 67.

▶ Make the Base

Cut a piece of core fiber, wrap it around the frame, and stab it in place. Use a thick needle to make the felting process quicker.

Stab small pieces of core fiber to the face in order to shape it gradually.

The wire frame allows you to manipulate the bear cub's arms. He can even hold objects, such as this bouquet of flowers.

Completed view after the entire body has been covered with core fiber. Use the core fiber to make the body more plump and to shape each body part.

▶ Add Color the Body

Separate some black wool roving, wrap it around the base, and stab to secure in place.

▶ Finish the Details

Stab all around the body to attach the wool roving and shape the body.

Once the entire body is covered in black wool roving, follow the individual project instructions to add the facial features and other details.

The following guide uses the Cockatiel on page 14 as an example.

▶ Make the Wire Frame

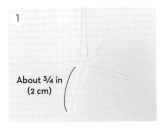

About ¾ in (2 cm)

Bend the floral wire to make a rough bird's foot shape. Each toe should be about ¾ in (2 cm) long.

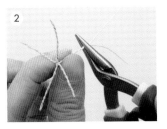

Using pliers, twist the two pieces of wire together from the base to the tip of each toe. Twist the wires together along the leg too.

▶ Wrap Embroidery Floss Around the Wire Frame

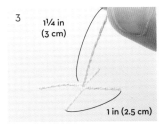

1¼ in (3 cm)

1 in (2.5 cm)

Trim the wire so that each toe is 1 in (2.5 cm) long and the leg is 1¼ in (3 cm) long.

Wrap pink embroidery floss around the wire frame from the base to the tip of the first toe.

Once you reach the tip, change direction and wrap toward the base. Follow this process to wrap the floss around the remaining toes and the leg.

Once you are finished wrapping, tie the embroidery floss in a tight knot.

SWAN BROOCH

SHOWN ON PAGE 6

MATERIALS

- **Wool roving**
  A bit of white
  A bit of brown
  A bit of orange
  A bit of black

- **A scrap of white sheet felt**

- **Brooch pin**

INSTRUCTIONS

1 Use the template on page 73 to cut the swan out of sheet felt. This will be the brooch base.

2 Stab white wool roving onto the brooch base, making the middle area plump to create the wings. Leave the beak area uncovered. ***See diagrams on page 73.***

3 Stab orange wool roving onto the beak, and then stab black wool roving onto the beak tip. ***See diagram on page 73.***

4 Roll a bit of brown wool roving between your fingertips to make an eye about the size of a sesame seed. Stab in place next to the beak.

5 Use the tip of the needle to form indented lines for the wings (refer to step 13 on page 44). ***Also see diagram on page 73.***

6 Sew a brooch pin to the back (refer to steps 25 – 26 on page 42).

FULL-SIZE PROJECT DIAGRAM

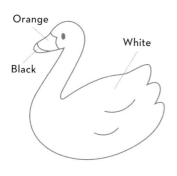

Orange

Black

White

②

STAB WHITE WOOL roving onto the brooch base (except for the beak). Make the middle area plump.

ADD A BIT more wool roving to the edges and stab into place using a fine gauge needle. Make sure that the felt is completely covered along the edges of the brooch.

Back

FLIP THE WORK over and secure any loose wool roving to the felt on the back of the brooch.

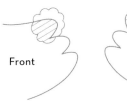

Front   Back

DON'T FORGET TO cover the tips of the tail feathers with a bit of wool roving, wrapping it around to the back of the brooch and stabbing in place.

Cut 1 of white sheet felt

FULL-SIZE TEMPLATE

❸

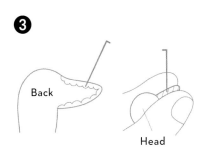

Back

Head

FOR A CLEAN finish, hold the beak between your fingers, wrap the wool roving around to the back of the brooch, and stab in place.

❺

STAB TO FORM indented lines for the wings.

HEDGEHOG BROOCH

SHOWN ON PAGE 7

MATERIALS

- **Wool roving**
  A bit of beige
  A bit of light brown
  A bit of brown
  A bit of black

- **A scrap of beige sheet felt**

- **Brooch pin**

INSTRUCTIONS

1 Use the template on page 75 to cut the hedgehog out of sheet felt. This will be the brooch base.

2 Stab light brown wool roving onto the brooch base, making the middle area plump to create a three-dimensional body. *See diagrams on page 75.*

3 Stab brown wool roving onto the hedgehog's back and side, leaving the head and belly uncovered. *See diagram on page 75.*

4 Roll a bit of beige wool roving between your fingertips until it is the shape of a grain of rice. Repeat this process to make several quills. Stab at both ends to attach the quills to the hedgehog's back and side. *See diagram on page 75.*

5 Follow the process used in steps 5–12 on pages 45–46 to make an ear out of light brown wool roving and attach it to the body. Add a bit of beige wool roving inside the ear. *See diagram on page 75.*

6 Cover the face and belly with a thin layer of beige wool roving, leaving the nose and legs uncovered. *See diagram on page 75.*

7 Use a bit of black wool roving to make the eye, nose, and mouth as shown in steps 17 and 18 on page 46. *Also see diagram on page 75.*

8 Sew a brooch pin to the back (refer to steps 25–26 on page 42).

FULL-SIZE PROJECT DIAGRAM

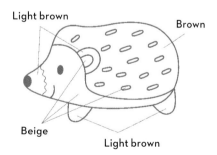

Light brown

Brown

Beige

Light brown

❷

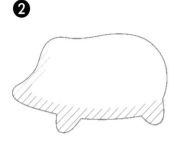

STAB LIGHT BROWN wool roving onto the brooch base. Make the middle area plump, especially the belly.

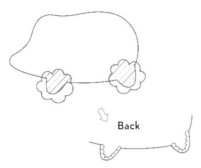

Back

ADD A BIT more loosened wool roving to the legs, wrapping it around to the back of the brooch and securing it in place.

Cut 1 of beige sheet felt

FULL-SIZE TEMPLATE

❸

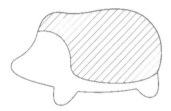

STAB BROWN WOOL roving to the hedgehog's back and side. This will be the area for the quills.

❹

Stab at both ends

STAB AT BOTH ends to attach the quills.

❺

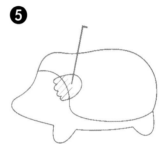

MAKE AN EAR out of light brown wool roving and attach it to the side of the head. Stab a bit of beige wool roving inside the ear.

❻

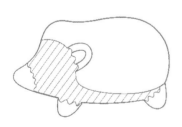

COVER THE FACE and belly with a thin layer of beige wool roving. Leave the nose and legs uncovered.

❼

Black

STAB SOME LOOSENED black wool roving to the tip of the nose. Roll beige wool roving into a rice grain-like shape with fingertips and stab in place to make the eye.

ROLL A THIN strip of black wool roving between your fingertips to make a rope, then stab it in place to make the mouth.

DONKEY BROOCH

SHOWN ON PAGE 7

MATERIALS

- **Wool roving**
  A bit of white
  A bit of dark gray
  A bit of black
  A bit of taupe
  A bit of brown

- **A scrap of beige sheet felt**

- **Brooch pin**

INSTRUCTIONS

1 Use the template on page 77 to cut the donkey out of sheet felt. This will be the brooch base.

2 Stab taupe wool roving onto the brooch base, making the middle area plump to create a three-dimensional body. Stab a bit of white wool roving to the nose and dark gray wool roving to the feet. *See diagram on page 77.*

3 Follow the process used in steps 37 – 41 on page 55 to make two large ears out of taupe, brown, and white wool roving. *Also see diagram on page 77.*

4 Attach the ears and mane. *See diagrams on page 77.*

5 Make and attach the tail. *See diagrams on page 77.*

6 Add a bit of white wool roving to the legs, just above the dark gray hooves. *See diagram on page 77.*

7 Use white and black wool roving to make the eye, as shown in steps 14 and 15 on page 44. Use black wool roving to make the mouth, as shown in step 18 on page 46, and a tiny bit of brown wool roving to make the nostril.

8 Sew a brooch pin to the back (refer to steps 25 – 26 on page 42).

FULL-SIZE PROJECT DIAGRAM

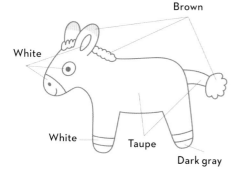

Brown

White

White

Taupe

Dark gray

❷

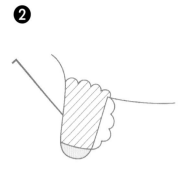

STAB TAUPE WOOL roving onto the brooch base. Make the middle area plump. Add a bit more loosened wool roving to the legs, wrapping it around to the back of the brooch and securing it in place.

❸

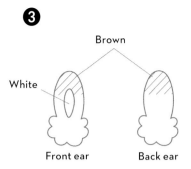

Brown

White

Front ear   Back ear

AFTER MAKING TWO ear shapes with taupe wool roving, stab a bit of brown wool roving to the tips. Stab a bit of white wool roving inside one of the ears. This will be the front ear.

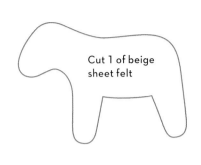

Cut 1 of beige sheet felt

❹

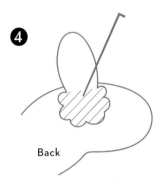

Back

STAB THE LOOSE fibers to attach the back ear to the back of the head.

USE YOUR FINGERTIPS to make a thin rope of brown wool roving for the mane. Stab to attach the mane, starting from the top of the head and continuing down the back. Leave the texture slightly fluffy.

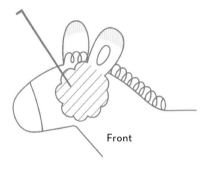

Front

STAB THE FRONT ear to the front of the head.

❺

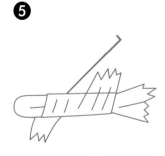

FOLD A BIT of brown wool roving in half so it is the desired length of the tail. Wrap a bit of taupe wool roving around it and stab to secure in place.

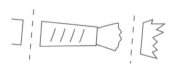

TRIM THE TAIL to the desired length, and then stab firmly to attach it to the back of the donkey's body.

❻

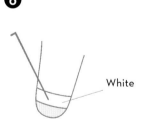

White

WRAP A BIT of white wool roving around the legs, just above the hooves and stab in place.

RABBIT BROOCH

SHOWN ON PAGE 6

MATERIALS

- **Wool roving**
  A bit of beige
  A bit of light brown
  A bit of brown
  A bit of dark brown

- **A scrap of beige sheet felt**

- **Brooch pin**

INSTRUCTIONS

1 Use the template on page 79 to cut the rabbit out of sheet felt. This will be the brooch base.

2 Stab light brown wool roving onto the brooch base, making the middle area plump to create a three-dimensional body. Leave the tail uncovered. **See diagram on page 79.**

3 Stab beige wool roving to the tail, stomach, and face. **See diagram on page 79.**

4 Follow the process used in steps 37–41 on page 55 to make two large ears out of light brown and beige wool roving and attach them to the head. **Also see diagrams on page 79.**

5 Make the remaining back leg out of light brown wool roving and attach it to the body. Add a bit of loosened light brown wool roving to the leg joints to build up the haunches. **See diagram on page 79.**

6 Make two small front legs out of light brown wool roving and attach to the upper body.

7 Add a bit of beige wool roving to the chest. **See diagram on page 79.**

8 Use a bit of brown wool roving to make the nose and dark brown wool roving to make the eye and mouth, as shown on page 38.

9 Stab a bit of loosened light brown wool roving to the back. **See diagram on page 79.**

10 Sew a brooch pin to the back (refer to steps 25–26 on page 42).

FULL-SIZE PROJECT DIAGRAM

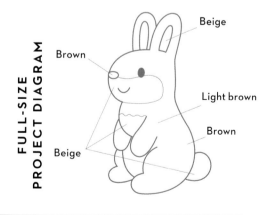

Beige

Brown

Light brown

Brown

Beige

2

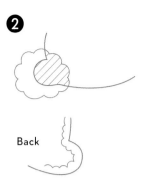

Back

STAB LIGHT BROWN wool roving onto the brooch base. Make the middle area plump. Add a bit more loosened wool roving to the leg, wrapping it around to the back of the brooch and securing it in place.

3

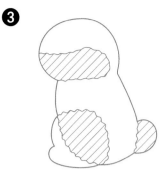

STAB LOOSENED BEIGE wool roving to the tail, stomach, and face. Fold the extra wool roving to the back and secure it in place.

Cut 1 of beige sheet felt

4

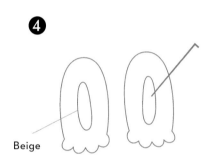

Beige

AFTER MAKING TWO ears with light brown wool roving, add beige wool roving inside both ears.

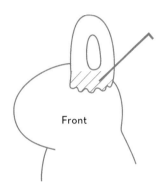

Front

STAB THE LOOSE fibers to attach one ear to the front of the head.

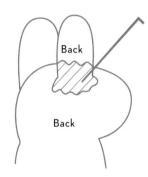

Back

Back

STAB THE LOOSE fibers to attach the remaining ear to the back of the head.

5

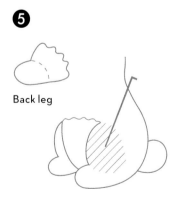

Back leg

AFTER ATTACHING THE remaining back leg to the body, add a bit of loosened light brown wool roving to the leg joints.

7

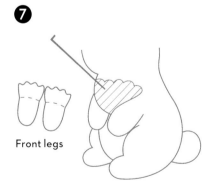

Front legs

AFTER ATTACHING THE front legs, stab some beige wool roving to the chest.

9

STAB SOME LOOSENED light brown wool roving to the back.

RABBIT BROOCH　**79**

MUSHROOM BROOCH

SHOWN ON PAGE 7

MATERIALS

- Wool roving
  A bit of white
  A bit of beige
  A bit of red
  A bit of orange

- A scrap of white sheet felt

- Brooch pin

INSTRUCTIONS

Refer to pages 40–42 for step-by-step photos and detailed instructions for making the Mushroom Brooch.

COLOR KEY

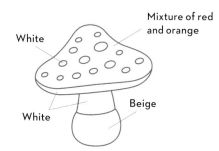

White

Mixture of red and orange

White

Beige

FULL-SIZE TEMPLATE

Cut 1 of white sheet felt

WHITE-EYE BROOCH

SHOWN ON PAGE 6

MATERIALS

- Wool roving
  A bit of white
  A bit of brown
  A bit of light green
  A bit of yellow
  A bit of dark green
- A scrap of white sheet felt
- Brooch pin

INSTRUCTIONS

Refer to pages 43–44 for step-by-step photos and detailed instructions for making the White-Eye Brooch.

COLOR KEY

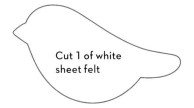

Mixture of light green and yellow
Brown
Mixture of light green and dark green
Yellow
White
Dark green

FULL-SIZE TEMPLATE

Cut 1 of white sheet felt

CHIPMUNK BROOCH

SHOWN ON PAGE 7

MATERIALS

- Wool roving
  A bit of white
  A bit of light brown
  A bit of brown
  A bit of dark brown
- A scrap of beige sheet felt
- Brooch pin

INSTRUCTIONS

Refer to pages 45–47 for step-by-step photos and detailed instructions for making the Chipmunk Brooch.

COLOR KEY

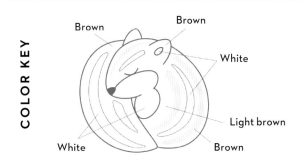

Brown
Brown
White
Light brown
White
Brown

FULL-SIZE TEMPLATE

Cut 1 of beige sheet felt

GREAT TIT

SHOWN ON PAGE 9

MATERIALS

- Wool roving
  A bit of white
  A bit of dark gray
  A bit of sage green
  A bit of black
  A bit of gray

- A scrap of dark brown sheet felt

- Two 4 mm black eye buttons

INSTRUCTIONS

After making the head and body as shown in steps 1–16 on pages 48–49, follow steps 17–48 on pages 49–51 to complete the Great Tit.

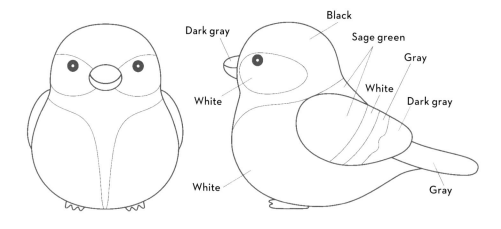

Dark gray

Black

Sage green

Gray

White

White

Dark gray

White

Gray

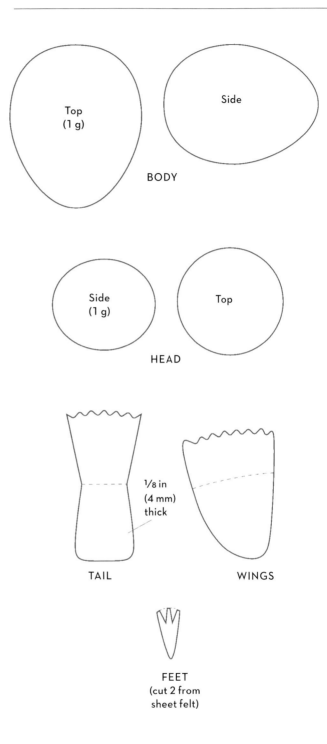

Top
(1 g)

Side

BODY

Side
(1 g)

Top

HEAD

1/8 in
(4 mm)
thick

TAIL

WINGS

FEET
(cut 2 from
sheet felt)

WHITE-EYE

SHOWN ON PAGE 9

MATERIALS

- **Wool roving**
  A bit of white
  A bit of moss green
  A bit of brown
  A bit of green
  A bit of yellow

- **A scrap of dark brown sheet felt**

- **Two 3 mm black eye buttons**

INSTRUCTIONS

1 Refer to steps 1–16 on pages 48–49 for step-by-step photos and detailed instructions for making the head and body. Use the templates on page 83 as a guide.

2 Use green wool roving to make and attach the tail, as shown in steps 19–24 on page 49.

3 Add white wool roving underneath the base of the tail, as shown in steps 25–26 on page 50.

4 Stab a bit of loosened moss green wool roving from the neck down to the base of the tail, as shown in step 27 on page 50.

5 Add some loosened moss green wool roving to the head and neck. **See diagram on page 85.**

6 Use green wool roving to make and attach the wings, as shown in steps 28–34 on page 50.

7 Use moss green wool roving to add shading to the wings. **See diagrams on page 85.**

8 Add moss green wool roving to the neck and cheeks to make them plump.

9 Add a light layer of loosened white wool roving to the chest, as shown in step 39 on page 51.

10 Add a bit of yellow wool roving to the chest.

11 Use brown wool roving to make the beak, then add a dividing line of white wool roving, as shown in steps 41–43 on page 51.

12 Stab bits of white wool roving onto the head to create circle shapes for the eyes. Next, attach the eye buttons as shown in steps 44–46 on page 51.

13 Make and attach the feet as shown in steps 47–48 on page 51.

Brown

Moss green

Yellow

Moss green

White

Green

❺

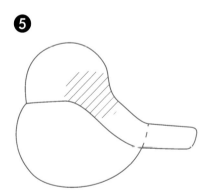

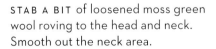

STAB A BIT of loosened moss green wool roving to the head and neck. Smooth out the neck area.

❼

STAB A THIN layer of loosened moss green wool roving to the wing, starting at the base and leaving the tip of the wing uncovered.

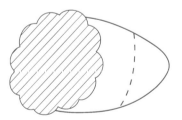

STAB A BIT more loosened moss green wool roving to the wing, starting at the base and stopping mid-wing. This will create shading.

WHITE-TAILED SPARROW

SHOWN ON PAGE 9

MATERIALS

- **Wool roving**
  A bit of rust
  A bit of beige
  A bit of white
  A bit of brown
  A bit of light brown
  A bit of dark brown

- **A scrap of dark brown sheet felt**

- **Two 3 mm black eye buttons**

INSTRUCTIONS

1 Use beige wool roving to make the head and body, as shown in steps 1–16 on pages 48–49. Use the templates on page 83 as a guide.

2 Use brown wool roving to make and attach the tail, as shown in steps 19–24 on page 49. ***Also see diagram on page 87.***

3 Add white wool roving underneath the base of the tail, as shown in steps 25–26 on page 50.

4 Stab a bit of loosened light brown wool roving from the neck down to the base of the tail, as shown in step 27 on page 50.

5 Use brown wool roving to make and attach the wings, as shown in steps 28–34 on page 50.

6 Use rust and light brown wool roving to add shading to the wings. ***See diagram on page 87.***

7 Use white, rust, and dark brown wool roving to add a pattern to the wings. ***See diagrams on page 87.***

8 Add white wool roving to plump up the neck and cheeks.

9 Add a light layer of loosened beige wool roving to the chest, as shown in step 39 on page 51.

10 Add a triangle of dark brown wool roving to the face. Use the Full-Size Project Diagram on page 87 as a guide. ***Also see diagram on page 87.***

11 Use brown wool roving to make the beak, then add a dividing line of white wool roving, as shown in steps 41–43 on page 51.

12 Add dark brown circles to the cheeks.

13 Attach the eye buttons as shown in steps 44–46 on page 51.

14 Make and attach the feet as shown in steps 47–48 on page 51.

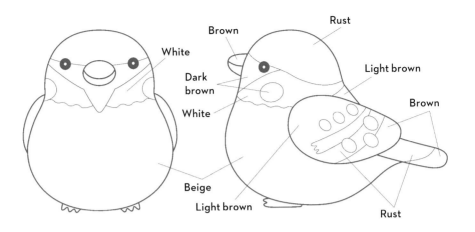

2

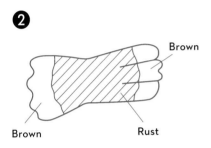

MAKE THE TAIL with brown wool roving. Add some rust wool roving, leaving the tip uncovered and the fibers loose at the base of the tail. Use the tip of the needle to make indented lines.

6

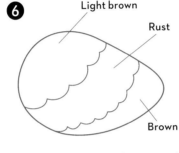

STAB A THIN layer of rust wool roving to the wings, starting at the base, leaving ⅓ of each wing uncovered. Next, stab some light brown wool roving to the wings, starting at the base and stopping after covering ⅓ of each wing.

7

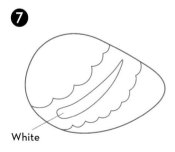

STAB A THIN line of white wool roving to the middle of each wing.

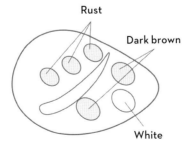

ROLL BITS OF wool roving into balls and stab to the wings to create a pattern as shown above.

10

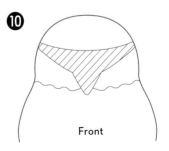

AFTER MARKING THE eye placement with pins, add dark brown wool roving to the face. Use the Full-Size Project Diagram above as a guide.

RABBIT

SHOWN ON PAGE 10

MATERIALS

- **Wool roving**
  A bit of white
  A bit of light brown
  A bit of brown
  A bit of dark brown

INSTRUCTIONS

Refer to pages 52–55 for step-by-step photos and detailed instructions for making the Rabbit.

FULL-SIZE PROJECT DIAGRAM

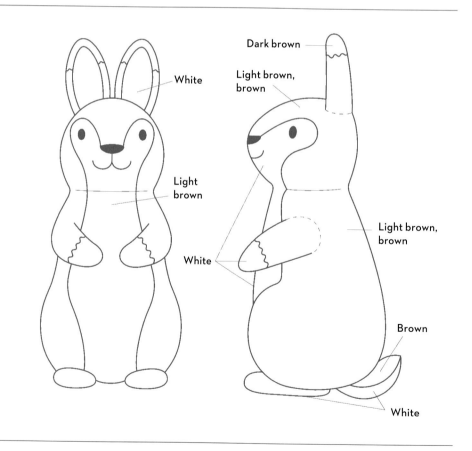

White

Light brown

White

Dark brown

Light brown, brown

Light brown, brown

Brown

White

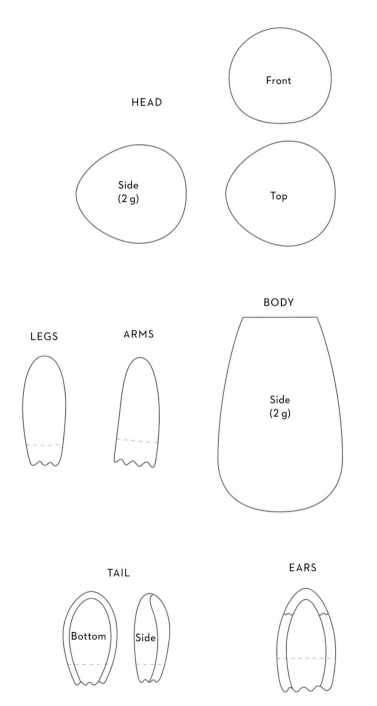

HEAD

Front

Side
(2 g)

Top

BODY

LEGS

ARMS

Side
(2 g)

TAIL

Bottom

Side

EARS

SQUIRREL

SHOWN ON PAGE 11

MATERIALS

- **Wool roving**
  A bit of brown
  A bit of white
  A bit of light brown
  A bit of black
  A bit of dark brown

- **Light brown embroidery floss**

INSTRUCTIONS

1 Use brown wool roving to make the head, as shown in step 1 on page 52. Use the templates on page 91 as a guide.

2 Use brown wool roving to make the body, as shown in steps 2 – 6 on page 52. Use the template on page 91 as a guide.

3 Attach the head and body, then add a bit more brown wool roving to the neck to smooth out the shape, as shown in steps 7 – 11 on page 52. *Also see diagram on page 92.*

FULL-SIZE PROJECT DIAGRAM

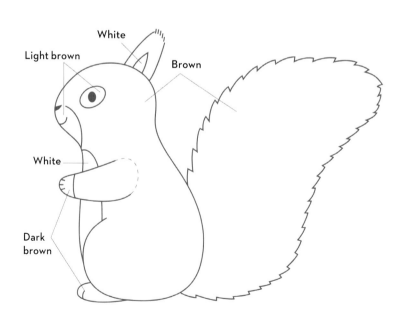

White

Light brown

Brown

White

Dark brown

4. Add a bit of loosened brown wool roving to the haunches, back, and cheeks to make them more plump. *See diagram on page 92.*

5. Stab a bit of loosened white wool roving to the belly and bottom and a bit of loosened light brown wool roving to the mouth. *See diagram on page 92.*

6. Make two ears out of brown wool roving, then add a bit of white wool roving to the inside. Attach the ears to the head. *See diagrams on pages 92–93.*

7. Make two paws out of dark brown wool roving, using the template at right as a guide. Next, stab a bit of brown wool roving to each paw to form the arms, leaving about ¼ in (5 mm) of the paws uncovered at the tips. *See diagrams on page 93.* Use light brown embroidery floss to embroider three claws on each paw, as shown in steps 13–20 on page 63.

8. Make two legs out of dark brown wool roving, using the template at right as a guide. Embroider four claws on each leg.

9. Attach the arms and legs to the body, as shown in steps 22–26 on pages 53–54.

10. Make the tail and attach it to the body, as shown on page 56.

11. Stab a bit of loosened light brown wool roving to the area around the eyes. Use black wool roving to make the eyes and dark brown wool roving to make the nose and mouth as shown on page 38. *Also see diagram on page 93.*

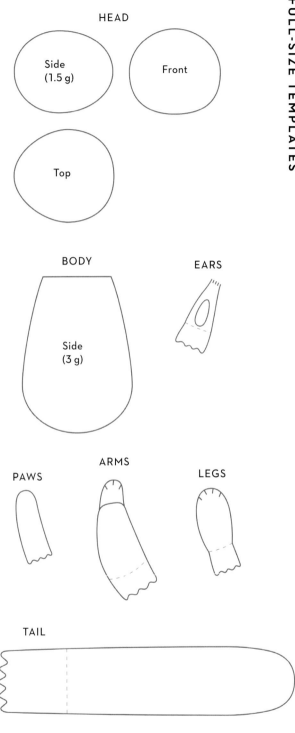

HEAD

Side (1.5 g)

Front

Top

BODY

Side (3 g)

EARS

PAWS

ARMS

LEGS

TAIL

❸

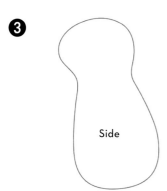

Side

USE PINS TO temporarily attach the head and body, then follow steps 7–11 on page 52 to permanently attach. Add a bit more wool roving to the neck and back and felt into shape as shown in the diagram above.

❹

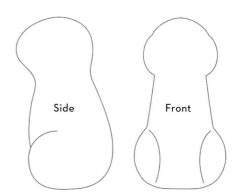

Side   Front

ADD WOOL ROVING to the haunches, back, and cheeks to make them more plump.

❺

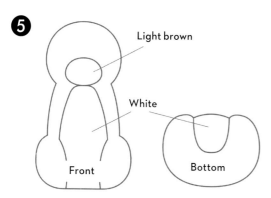

Light brown

White

Front   Bottom

ADD WHITE WOOL roving to the belly and bottom and light brown wool roving to the mouth.

❻

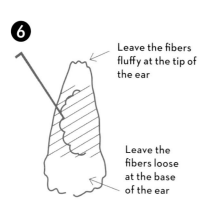

Leave the fibers fluffy at the tip of the ear

Leave the fibers loose at the base of the ear

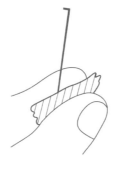

Fluffy tip

White wool roving

MAKE TWO EARS, as shown in steps 37–40 on page 55. Leave the fibers fluffy at the tips of the ears.

HOLD EACH EAR between your fingers and stab the edges to form into shape.

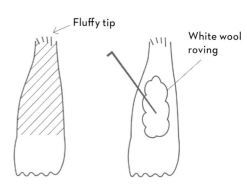

STAB A BIT of loosened white wool roving inside each ear.

USE PINS TO temporarily attach the ears to the head. Once you are happy with the placement, stab the loose fibers at the base of each ear to permanently attach.

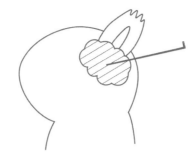

STAB A BIT of loosened brown wool roving to the base of each ear.

7

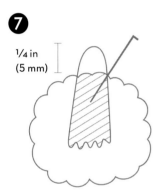

¼ in (5 mm)

STAB A BIT of brown wool roving to the paws, leaving about ¼ in (5 mm) uncovered at the tips.

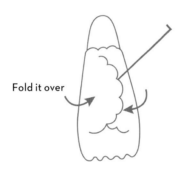

Fold it over

WRAP THE WOOL roving around the edges to the back of the arm. Stab to secure in place. Make two arms.

11

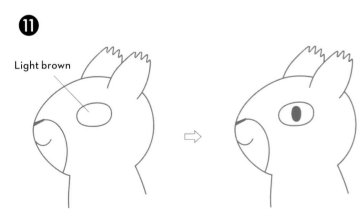

Light brown

STAB A BIT of light brown wool roving around the eyes. Make the eyes with black wool roving and the nose and mouth with dark brown wool roving.

DONKEY

SHOWN ON PAGE 12

MATERIALS

- **Wool roving**
  A bit of brown
  A bit of white
  A bit of dark gray
  A bit of light brown
  A bit of black

INSTRUCTIONS

1 Refer to steps 1 – 16 on pages 57 – 58 for step-by-step photos and detailed instructions for making the head, body, and legs. Use the templates on page 97 as a guide.

2 Follow the process used in steps 37 – 41 on page 55 to make two ears out of brown wool roving. Use the template on page 97 as a guide. Stab a bit of gray wool roving to the tips and white wool roving to the inside. Fold the ears at the base and attach to the head. **See diagrams on page 96.**

3 Make the mane. **See diagrams on page 96.**

4 Stab a bit of light brown wool roving onto the head to create circle shapes for the eyes. Next, roll bits of black wool roving into balls about the size of sesame seeds and stab in place at the center of the circles.

5 Use brown wool roving to make the nostrils and dark brown wool roving to make the mouth, as shown on page 38.

6 Use brown and dark gray wool roving to make the tail, using the template on page 97 as a guide. **See diagrams on page 96.**

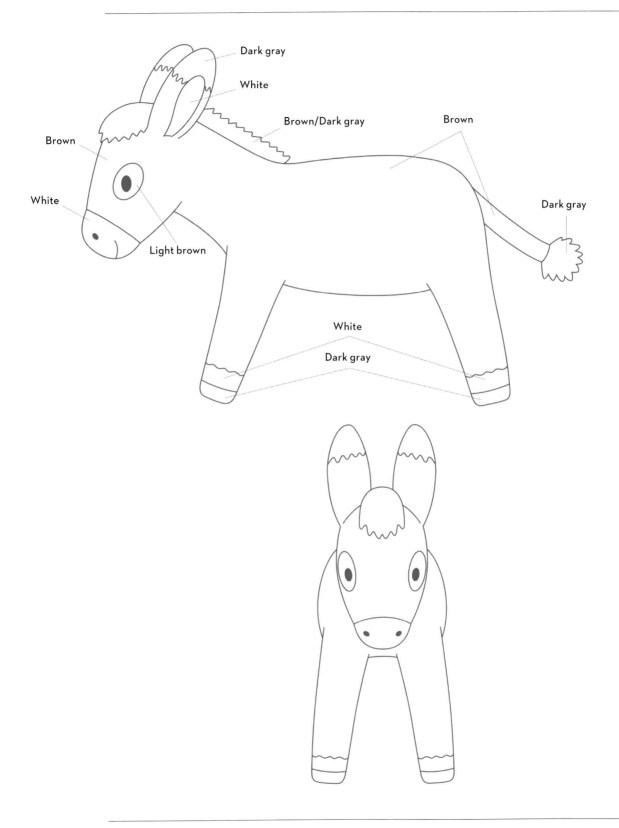

Dark gray

White

Brown/Dark gray

Brown

Brown

Dark gray

White

Light brown

Dark gray

White

White

Dark gray

2

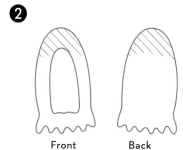

Front   Back

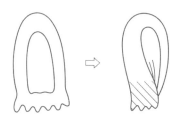

MAKE TWO EARS, as shown in steps 37–41 on page 55. Add a bit of dark gray wool roving to the tips of the ears and white wool roving inside the ears.

FOLD THE BASE of each ear vertically and fasten to the head with pins. Stab the loose fibers at the base to the head to permanently attach.

3

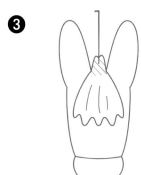

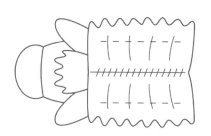

MAKE A SMALL bundle of brown wool roving and stab to attach it to the forehead. Next, make a small bundle of dark gray wool roving and stab to attach it on top of the brown. Trim into shape.

MAKE A BUNDLE of brown wool roving and stab to attach it to the donkey's neck in a straight line. Repeat with a bundle of dark gray wool roving.

COMPLETED VIEW OF the mane featuring both colors of wool roving. Trim the mane short.

6

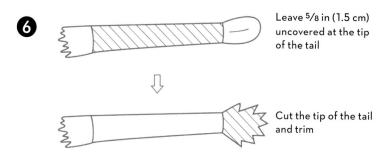

Leave ⅝ in (1.5 cm) uncovered at the tip of the tail

Cut the tip of the tail and trim

FOLD THE DARK gray wool roving in half and wrap it with brown wool roving. Cut the tip of the tail at the fold and trim into shape.

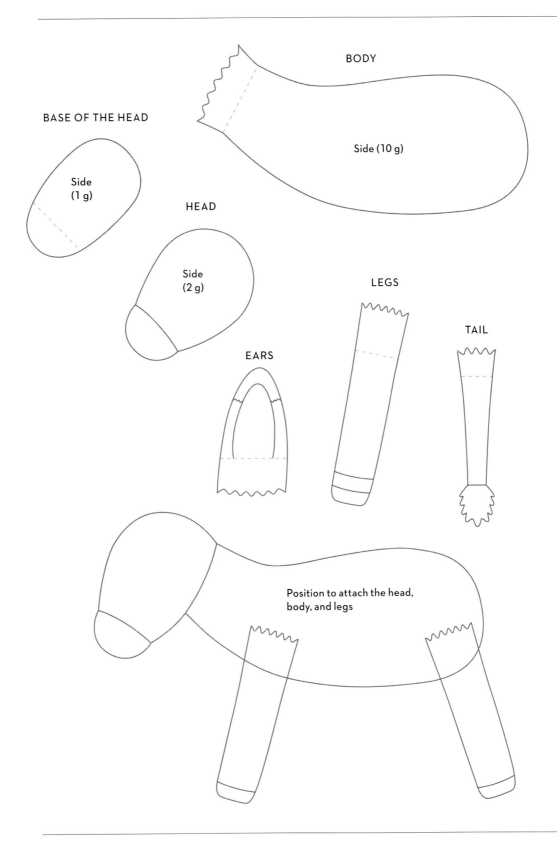

BASE OF THE HEAD

Side (1 g)

BODY

Side (10 g)

HEAD

Side (2 g)

LEGS

TAIL

EARS

Position to attach the head, body, and legs

HEDGEHOG

SHOWN ON PAGE 13

MATERIALS

- Wool roving
  A bit of taupe
  A bit of white
  A bit of dark gray
  A bit of black
- Chunky weight wool/alpaca yarn in brown, such as Hamanaka Sonomono Alpaca Wool
- Light brown embroidery floss

INSTRUCTIONS

1. Use taupe wool roving to make the head, as shown in step 1 on page 52. Use the template on page 99 as a guide.

2. Use taupe wool roving to make the body, as shown in steps 2–6 on page 52. Use the template on page 99 as a guide.

3. Attach the head and body, then add a bit more taupe wool roving to the neck to smooth out the shape, as shown in steps 7–11 on page 52.

FULL-SIZE PROJECT DIAGRAM

Taupe

White

Brown yarn

Dark gray

4. Add a bit of loosened taupe wool roving to the head to make a pointy nose. Next, add more taupe wool roving to the belly to give the body a gourd shape. **See diagrams on page 100.**

5. Use the felting needle to insert pieces of yarn into the head, back, and bottom to create the quills. Trim into shape. **See diagrams on page 100.**

6. Use the felting needle to insert the ends of the yarn into the wool roving along the hairline. **See diagram on page 101.**

7. Make two ears out of taupe wool roving, then add a bit of white wool roving to the inside. Use the template at right as a guide. Attach the ears to the head along the hairline. **See diagram on page 101.**

8. Stab loosened white wool roving to the face and belly, leaving the tip of the nose uncovered. See diagram on page 101.

9. Make two arms and two legs using dark gray wool, then embroider three claws on each, as shown in steps 13–20 on page 63. Use the templates at right as a guide.

10. Attach the arms and legs to the body. Add a bit of loosened taupe wool roving to the base of the arms.

11. Stab a bit of loosened white wool roving onto the head to create circles for the eyes. Next, roll bits of black wool roving into balls and stab into place at the center of the white circles. **See diagram on page 101.** Make the nose and mouth with black wool roving, as shown on page 38.

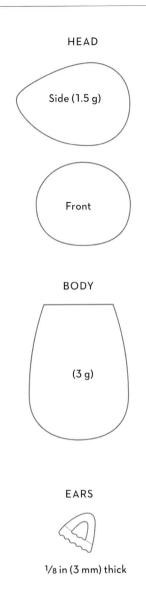

HEAD

Side (1.5 g)

Front

BODY

(3 g)

EARS

⅛ in (3 mm) thick

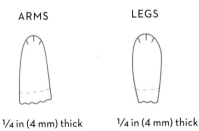

ARMS

LEGS

¼ in (4 mm) thick ¼ in (4 mm) thick

4

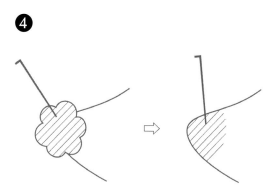

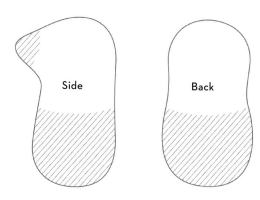

GRADUALLY ADD BITS of loosened taupe wool roving to form the nose into a pointed shape.

ADD TAUPE WOOL roving to the belly to give the body a nice, round gourd shape.

5

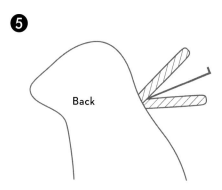

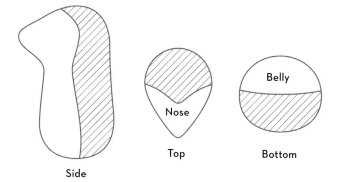

CUT 3-4 IN (8-10 cm) long pieces of yarn. Fold each piece in half and stab it at the center to embed the yarn into the wool roving. The yarn should not come out when pulled slightly.

EMBED YARN ALONG the areas shaded in the above diagrams. This will create quills along the head, back, and bottom.

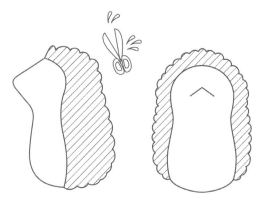

CUT THE EXCESS yarn and trim the quills into shape.

6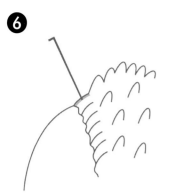

INSERT THE YARN ends into the wool roving along the hairline.

7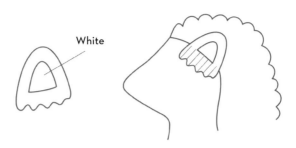

MAKE TWO EARS out of taupe wool roving. Add a bit of white wool roving to the inside. Stab to attach the ears along the hairline, between the quills and the face.

8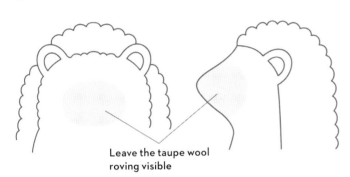

Leave the taupe wool roving visible

STAB LOOSENED WHITE wool roving lightly over the face and belly, leaving the tip of the nose uncovered.

11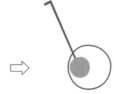

STAB LOOSENED WHITE wool roving onto the head to make circles for the eyes.

ROLL BITS OF black wool roving into balls and stab in place at the center of the white circles.

COCKATIEL

SHOWN ON PAGE 14

MATERIALS

- Wool roving
  A bit of brown
  A bit of beige
  A bit of pink
  A bit of orange
  A bit of red
  A bit of yellow
  A bit of light yellow
  A bit of white

- Pink embroidery floss

- Two ⅛ in (3 mm) black eye buttons

- 28-gauge white floral wire

INSTRUCTIONS

1 Use light yellow wool roving to make the head, as shown in steps 1–5 on page 48. Use the templates on page 105 as a guide.

2 Use white wool roving to make the body, as shown in steps 6–9 on page 48. Use the templates on page 105 as a guide.

FULL-SIZE PROJECT DIAGRAM

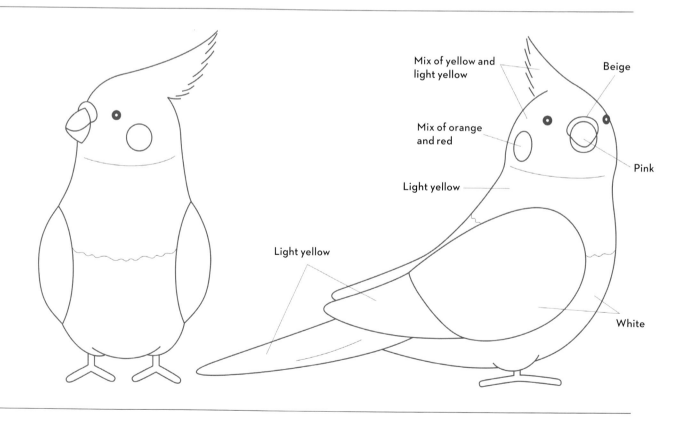

Mix of yellow and light yellow

Beige

Mix of orange and red

Pink

Light yellow

Light yellow

White

3 Attach the head and body, then add a bit more white wool roving to smooth out the neck, as shown in steps 10 – 14 on pages 48 – 49. Add a bit of light yellow wool roving to the neck.

4 Use white wool roving to make the tail, using the template on page 105 as a guide. Add light yellow wool roving to the tip of the tail to create shading, as shown in steps 6 – 7 on page 43.

5 Attach the tail to the body. Add a bit of white wool roving to the base for support, as shown in steps 25 – 26 on page 50.

6 Use white wool roving to make two wings, using the template on page 105 as a guide. Just like with the tail, add light yellow wool roving to the tips of the wings to create shading.

7 Attach the wings to the body. Add a bit of loosened white wool roving to the base of the wings to help smooth out the shape.

8 Stab a bit of loosened light yellow wool to the chest and back. *See diagram on page 104.*

9 Use pink wool roving to make the beak, as shown in steps 41 – 42 on page 51.

10 Stab a bit of light yellow wool to the cheeks to make them plump. *See diagram on page 104.*

11 Mix yellow and light yellow wool roving in a 1 : 1 ratio (refer to page 41 for instructions on mixing colors of wool roving). Use the mixed wool roving to make the crest. *See diagrams on page 104.*

12 Stab more of the mixed wool roving from step 11 onto the face.

13 Mix orange and red wool roving in a 1 : 1 ratio. Stab bits of this mixed wool roving onto the face to create circle shapes for the cheeks.

14 Use beige wool roving to make the nose, directly above the beak. Use the felting needle to make two holes in the nose for nostrils. *See diagram on page 104.*

15 Use a thin rope of brown wool roving to divide the beak in two, as shown in step 43 on page 51.

16 Attach the black eye buttons.

17 Use floral wire and pink embroidery floss to make the legs, as shown on page 71.

18 Insert the legs into the body. Add a bit of white wool roving at the base of the legs. *See diagrams on page 104.*

8

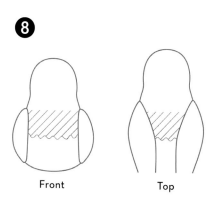

Front   Top

STAB LOOSENED LIGHT yellow wool roving to the chest and back, between the wings.

10

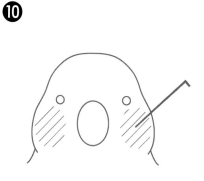

ADD LIGHT YELLOW wool roving on each side of the beak to make the cheeks plump.

11

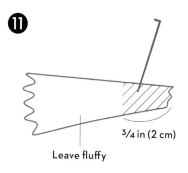

¾ in (2 cm)

Leave fluffy

MIX YELLOW AND light yellow wool roving in a 1:1 ratio. Make a small bundle and stab at one end for about ¾ in (2 cm) to create the crest.

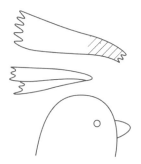

FOLD A TUFT of the mixed wool roving in half. Layer this folded tuft and the crest on top of the head and stab above the beak to secure.

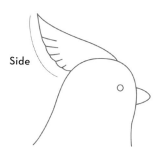

Side

CUT THE EXCESS wool roving and trim into a crest shape.

14

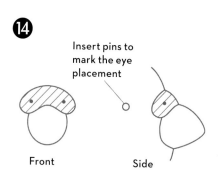

Insert pins to mark the eye placement

Front   Side

STAB A BIT of beige wool roving to the face, just above the beak. Use the felting needle to make two nostrils.

18

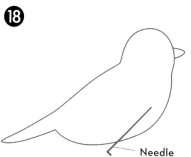

Needle

INSERT THE FELTING needle into the chest to make holes at the positions to attach the legs.

INSERT THE LEGS into the holes. It is not necessary to use glue. Add a bit of white wool roving around the legs.

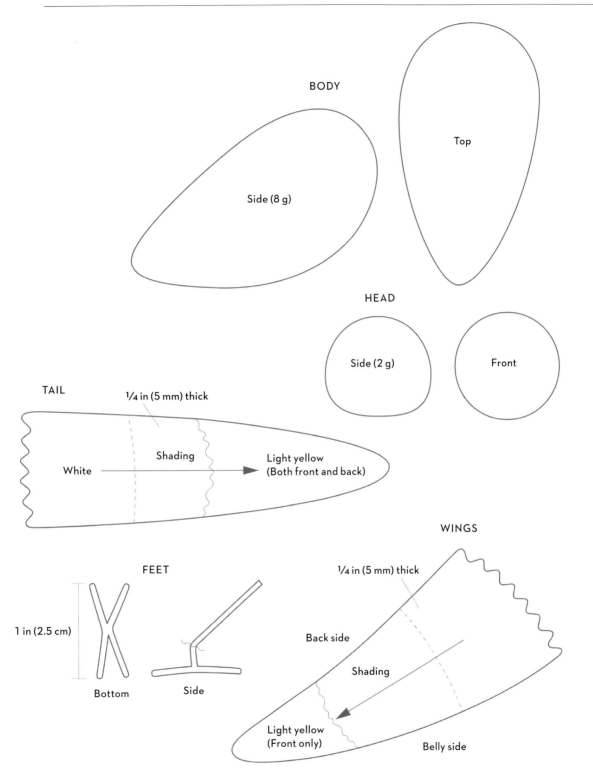

BODY

Top

Side (8 g)

HEAD

Side (2 g)

Front

TAIL

¼ in (5 mm) thick

Shading

White

Light yellow
(Both front and back)

FEET

WINGS

¼ in (5 mm) thick

1 in (2.5 cm)

Back side

Shading

Bottom

Side

Light yellow
(Front only)

Belly side

KITTEN

SHOWN ON PAGE 16

MATERIALS

- **Wool roving**
  A bit of white
  A bit of dark gray
  A bit of light brown
  A bit of gray
  A bit of black

- **Light brown embroidery floss**

INSTRUCTIONS

Refer to pages 62–66 for step-by-step photos and detailed instructions for making the Kitten. Use the templates on page 107.

FULL-SIZE PROJECT DIAGRAM

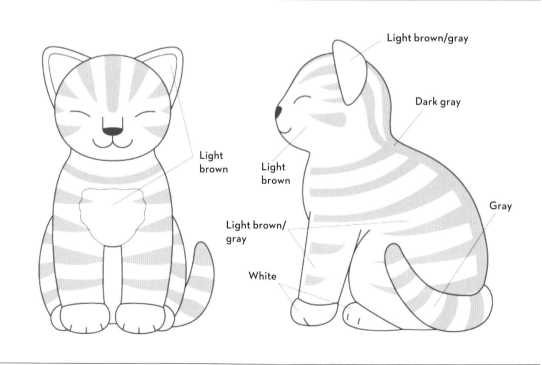

Light brown/gray

Dark gray

Light brown

Light brown

Gray

Light brown/gray

White

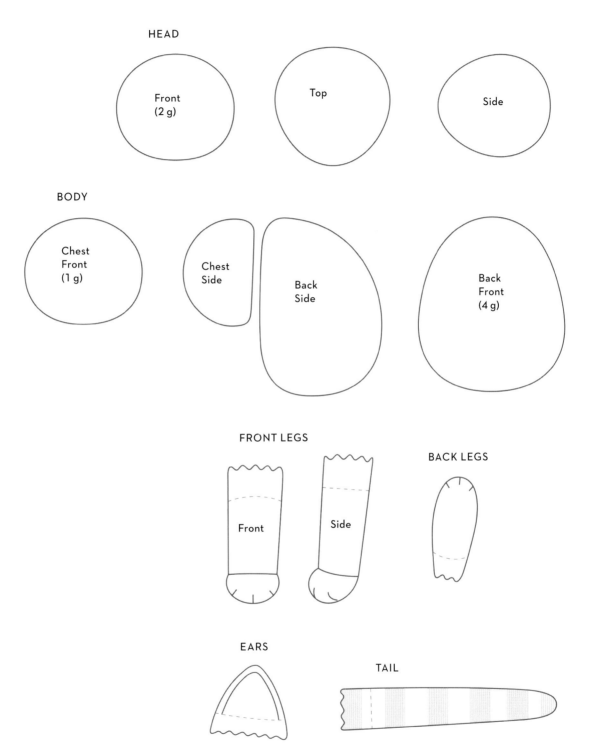

HEAD

Front
(2 g)

Top

Side

BODY

Chest
Front
(1 g)

Chest
Side

Back
Side

Back
Front
(4 g)

FRONT LEGS

Front

Side

BACK LEGS

EARS

TAIL

POODLE

SHOWN ON PAGE 18

MATERIALS

- **Wool roving**
  A bit of white
  A bit of dark brown

- **Curly wool locks**
  A bit of white

- **4–6 in (10–15 cm) of ¼ in (5 mm) wide ribbon**

INSTRUCTIONS

Refer to pages 59–61 for step-by-step photos and detailed instructions for making the Poodle. Use the templates on page 109.

FULL-SIZE PROJECT DIAGRAM

Curly wool locks

Head, body and legs
Base: White
Surface: Curly wool locks

Curly wool locks

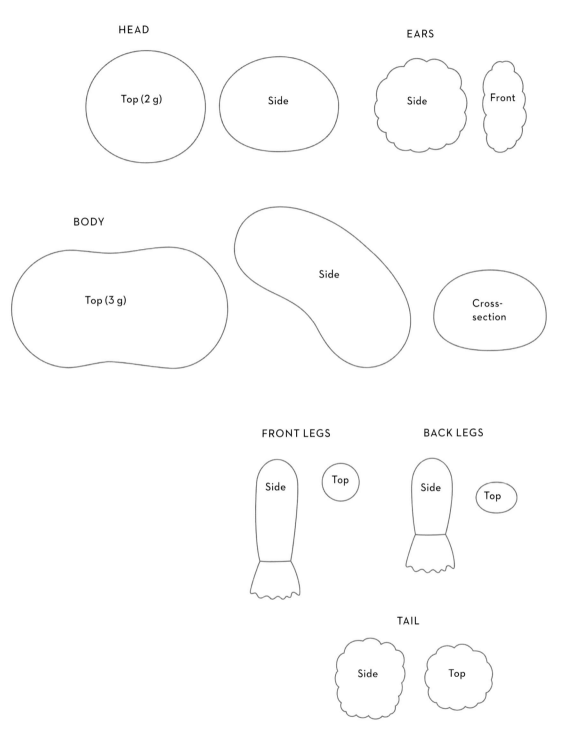

HEAD

Top (2 g)

Side

EARS

Side

Front

BODY

Top (3 g)

Side

Cross-section

FRONT LEGS

Side

Top

BACK LEGS

Side

Top

TAIL

Side

Top

SHIBA INU

SHOWN ON PAGE 18

MATERIALS

- **Wool roving**
  A bit of white
  A bit of light brown
  A bit of brown
  A bit of orange
  A bit of dark brown

- **Light brown embroidery floss**

INSTRUCTIONS

1 Use white wool roving to make the head, as shown in steps 1–5 on page 48. Use the template on page 113 as a guide.

2 Use white wool roving to make the chest and back separately, then attach them as shown in steps 2–8 on page 62. Use the templates on page 113 as a guide.

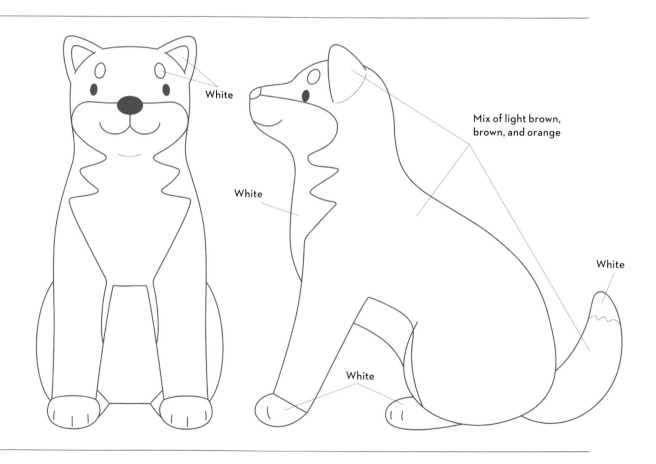

White

White

Mix of light brown, brown, and orange

White

White

White

FULL-SIZE PROJECT DIAGRAM

3 Attach the head and body, then add a bit more white wool roving to smooth out the neck, as shown in steps 9–10 on page 62.

4 Use white wool roving to make the snout. *See diagram on page 112.* Attach the snout to the head, adding a bit more white wool roving to smooth out the snout if necessary.

5 Use white wool roving to make the front legs. Use the templates on page 113 as a guide. Wrap with light brown wool roving and stab to secure in place. Embroider three claws on each front paw, as shown in steps 13–20 on page 63.

6 Attach the front legs to the body. Add a bit of loosened white wool roving to the base of the front legs.

7 Use white wool roving to make two haunches and attach to the sides of the body. Use the templates on page 113 as a guide. *See diagram on page 112.*

8 Make two back legs, following the process used for the front legs. Embroider four claws on each back paw. Attach the back legs to the body directly under the haunches.

9 Use pins to determine the placement of the eyes and nose. Stab light brown wool roving from the tip of the nose, along the back, legs, and tail. *See diagram on page 112.*

10 Mix brown and orange wool roving in a 2:1 ratio (refer to page 41 for instructions on mixing colors of wool roving).

11 Use the mixed wool roving to cover the light brown areas from step 9. Make jagged lines on the chest, as shown in the Full-Size Project Diagram on page 110.

12 Use the mixed wool roving to make two ears, then add a bit of white wool roving to the inside. Attach the ears to the head. Use the template on page 113 as a guide.

13 Use white wool roving to make the tail, then cover it with the mixed wool roving from step 10, leaving the tip of the tail uncovered. Use the template on page 113 as a guide. Form the tail into a slight curve and attach to the body. *See diagram on page 112.*

14 Use dark brown wool roving to make the eyes, nose, and mouth, as shown on page 38. Use white wool roving to make the eyebrows.

4

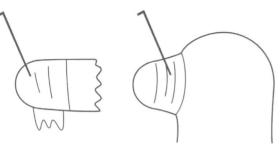

AFTER FOLDING THE white wool roving in half, wrap with more white wool roving and stab to shape into a snout. Attach to the face and smooth out.

7

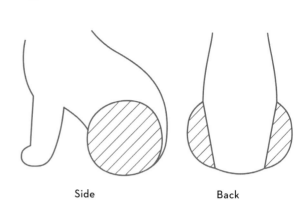

Side   Back

MAKE FLAT, BOWL-SHAPED haunches and attach to the sides of the body.

9

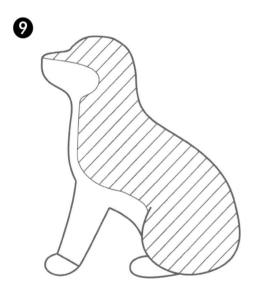

COVER THE BACK with light brown wool roving, from the tip of the nose to the bottom.

13

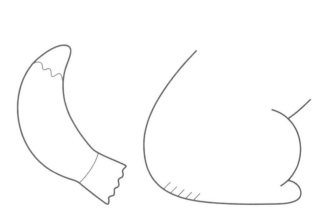

MAKE THE TAIL with white wool roving, then cover with the mixed wool roving, leaving the tip white. Give the tail a slight curve and stab it in place on the bottom.

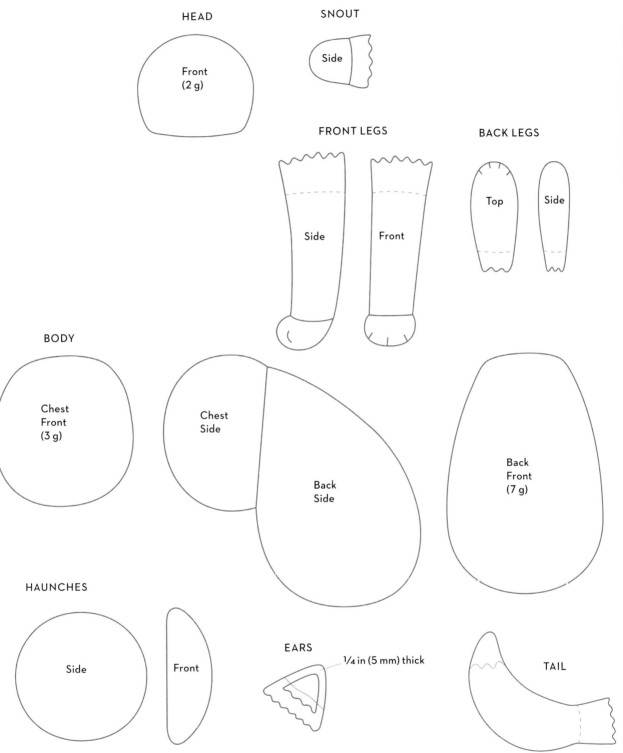

HEAD

SNOUT

Side

Front
(2 g)

FRONT LEGS

BACK LEGS

Side

Front

Top

Side

BODY

Chest
Front
(3 g)

Chest
Side

Back
Side

Back
Front
(7 g)

HAUNCHES

Side

Front

EARS

¼ in (5 mm) thick

TAIL

SHEEP

SHOWN ON PAGE 20

MATERIALS

- **Wool roving**
  A bit of white
  A bit of light brown
  A bit of brown
  A bit of pink
  A bit of black

- **Looped felting yarn in white**

- **19-gauge aluminum wire**

- **Sport weight yarn in off-white**

INSTRUCTIONS

Refer to pages 67–69 for step-by-step photos and detailed instructions for making the Sheep. Use the templates on page 115 as a guide.

FULL-SIZE PROJECT DIAGRAM

Pink

White

Base: White
Surface: White looped felting yarn

White

Light brown

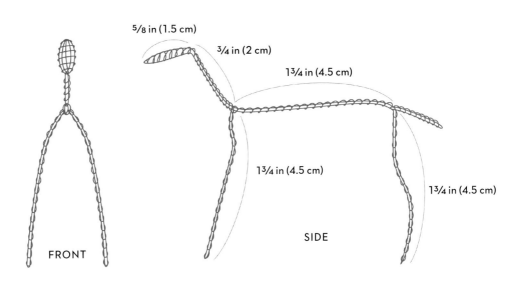

5/8 in (1.5 cm)

3/4 in (2 cm)

1³/4 in (4.5 cm)

1³/4 in (4.5 cm)

1³/4 in (4.5 cm)

FRONT

SIDE

EAR

1/8 in (3 mm) thick

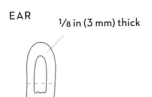

DEER

SHOWN ON PAGE 22

MATERIALS

- **Wool roving**
  A bit of white
  A bit of light brown
  A bit of brown
  A bit of dark rust
  A bit of beige
  A bit of dark brown
  A bit of rust

- **19-gauge aluminum wire**

- **Sport weight yarn in off-white**

INSTRUCTIONS

1 Make the wire frame, as shown in steps 1–7 on page 67. Use the template on page 119 as a guide.

2 Wrap the yarn around the wire frame, as shown in steps 8–9 on page 67.

FULL-SIZE PROJECT DIAGRAM (FOR FAWN)

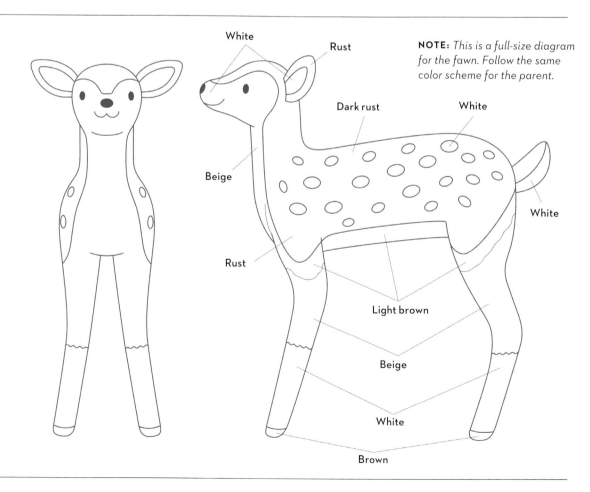

White

Rust

Dark rust

White

NOTE: *This is a full-size diagram for the fawn. Follow the same color scheme for the parent.*

Beige

White

Rust

Light brown

Beige

White

Brown

3 Wrap white wool roving around the frame and stab to form the head and body into shape, as shown in steps 10–13 on pages 67–68. Add a bit more white wool roving to the shoulders and bottom to make them plump. **See diagrams below.**

4 Make the hooves using brown wool roving, as shown in steps 14–16 on page 68. Make the legs thicker by wrapping with white wool roving and stabbing in place, as shown in step 17 on page 68.

5 Cover the head and body with beige wool roving, leaving the tip of the nose, lower legs, and tail white. **See diagram on page 118.**

6 Loosen a bit of light brown wool roving and attach just inside the layer of beige. You do not need to cover the back. **See diagram on page 118.**

7 Loosen a bit of rust wool roving and attach just inside the layer of light brown, covering the top of the head, body, back, and tail. **See diagram on page 118.**

8 Make two ears using rust wool roving, then add a bit of white wool roving to the inside. Attach the ears to the head. Use the template on page 119 as a guide. **See diagram on page 118.**

9 Add a thin, blurred line of dark rust wool roving down the back, from the head to the tail. **See diagram on page 118.**

10 Make the dots using white wool roving, as shown in steps 22–23 on page 42.

11 Use dark brown wool roving to make the eyes, nose, and mouth, as shown on page 38.

3

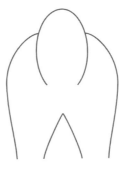

WRAP WHITE WOOL roving around the frame and stab into shape. Add loosened white wool roving to the face, shoulders, and bottom.

MAKE THE TAIL so it's flat when viewed from the side and round when viewed from behind.

5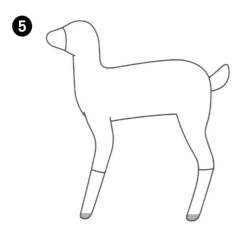

STAB BEIGE WOOL roving, leaving the tip of the nose, feet, and tail white.

6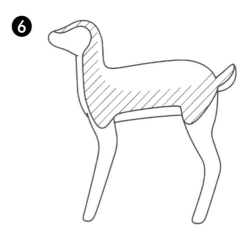

LOOSEN A BIT of light brown wool roving and stab just inside the beige layer. There's no need to cover the back.

7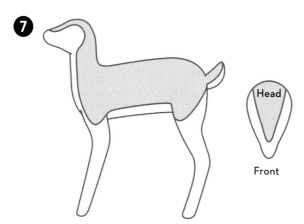

STAB RUST WOOL roving on top of the light brown wool roving, covering the top of the head, body, back, and tail.

8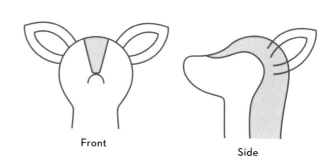

MAKE THE EARS, then stab white wool roving inside. Stab them from behind on the rust-colored part of the head.

9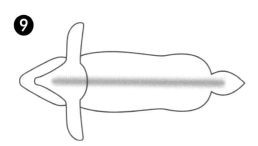

MAKE A THIN, blurred line with dark rust wool roving, starting from the head, down the back, and ending at the tail.

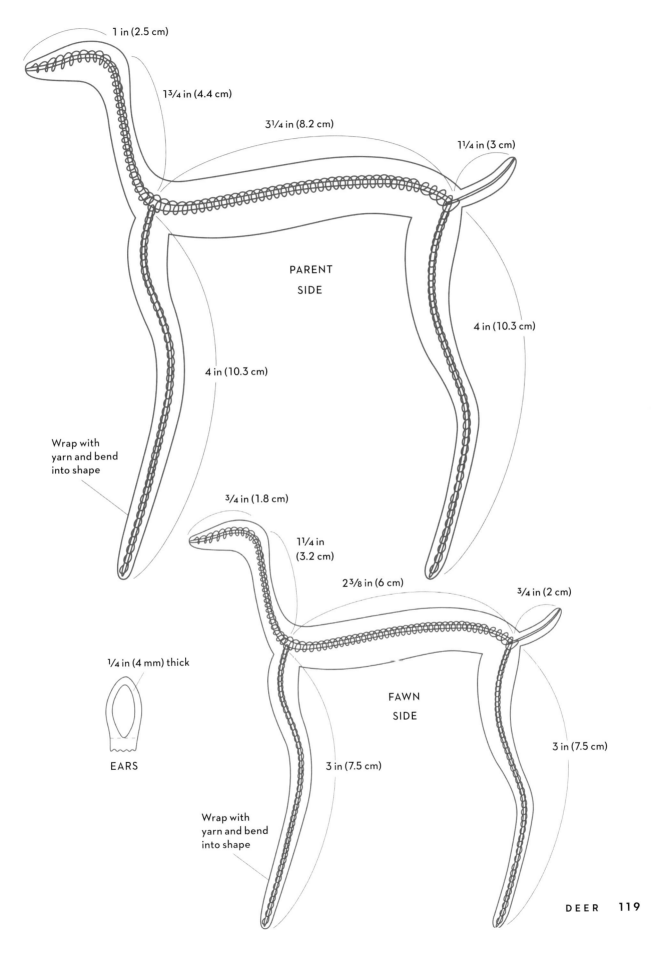

1 in (2.5 cm)

1³⁄₄ in (4.4 cm)

3¹⁄₄ in (8.2 cm)

1¹⁄₄ in (3 cm)

PARENT
SIDE

4 in (10.3 cm)

4 in (10.3 cm)

Wrap with
yarn and bend
into shape

³⁄₄ in (1.8 cm)

1¹⁄₄ in
(3.2 cm)

2³⁄₈ in (6 cm)

³⁄₄ in (2 cm)

¹⁄₄ in (4 mm) thick

FAWN
SIDE

3 in (7.5 cm)

EARS

3 in (7.5 cm)

Wrap with
yarn and bend
into shape

DEER   119

POLAR BEARS

SHOWN ON PAGE 24

MATERIALS

- Core fiber in white

- Wool roving
  A bit of gray
  A bit of white
  A bit of black

- 19-gauge aluminum wire

- Sport weight yarn in off-white

PROJECT DIAGRAM

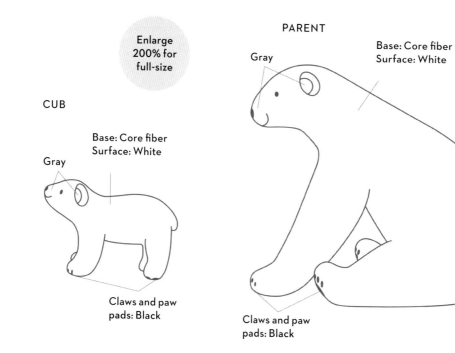

Enlarge 200% for full-size

PARENT

Gray

Base: Core fiber
Surface: White

Claws and paw
pads: Black

CUB

Base: Core fiber
Surface: White

Gray

Claws and paw
pads: Black

INSTRUCTIONS

1 Make the wire frame, as shown in steps 1 – 7 on page 67. Use the dimensions at right as a guide.

2 Wrap the yarn around the wire frame, as shown in step 8 on page 67.

3 Wrap the core fiber around the frame and stab in place, as shown in steps 3 – 5 on page 70.

4 Wrap white wool roving around the base and stab to secure in place and shape the body, as shown in steps 6 – 7 on page 70.

5 Felt the claws and paw pads using black wool roving.

6 Make two ears using white wool roving, then add a bit of gray wool roving to the inside. Attach the ears to the head, as shown in steps 22 – 24 on page 68.

7 Add a light layer of gray wool roving to the tip of the snout, then make the eyes, nose, and mouth using black wool roving, as shown on page 38.

8 Use white wool roving to make a small tail and attach to the bottom.

CUB

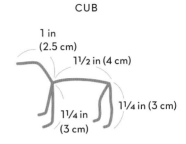

1 in (2.5 cm)
1½ in (4 cm)
1¼ in (3 cm)
1¼ in (3 cm)

PARENT

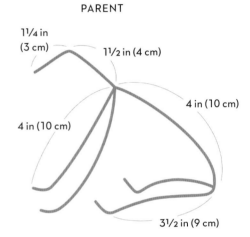

1¼ in (3 cm)
1½ in (4 cm)
4 in (10 cm)
4 in (10 cm)
3½ in (9 cm)

BEARS

SHOWN ON PAGE 26

MATERIALS

- Core fiber in white

- Wool roving
  A bit of white
  A bit of black
  A bit of beige
  A bit of pink

- 19-gauge aluminum wire

- Sport weight yarn in off-white

- Red and light brown embroidery floss (for the cubs only)

PROJECT DIAGRAM

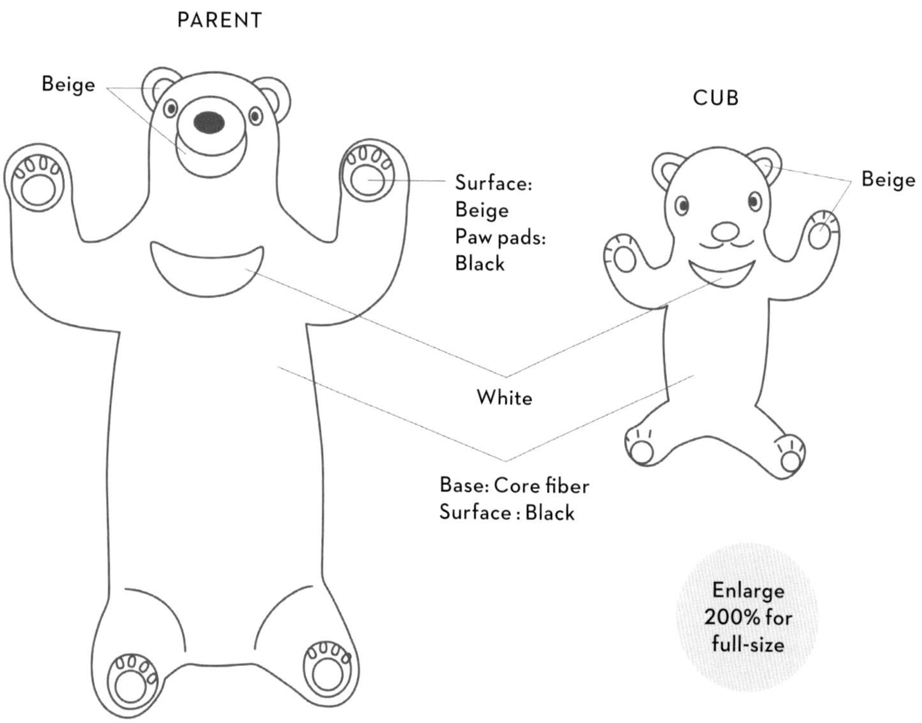

PARENT

Beige

CUB

Beige

Surface:
Beige
Paw pads:
Black

White

Base: Core fiber
Surface : Black

Enlarge
200% for
full-size

INSTRUCTIONS

1 Make the wire frame, as shown in steps 1–7 on page 67. Use the dimensions at right as a guide.

2 Wrap the yarn around the wire frame, as shown in step 8 on page 67.

3 Wrap the core fiber around the frame and stab in place, as shown in steps 3–5 on page 70.

4 Wrap black wool roving around the base and stab to secure in place and shape the body, as shown in steps 6–7 on page 70. For the parent, make the snout using beige wool roving.

5 Use loosened white wool roving to make the crescent moon-shaped pattern on the chest.

6 Add a bit of beige wool roving to the paws. Next, felt the claws and paw pads using black wool roving for the parent or embroider the claws with light brown embroidery floss for the cub, as shown in steps 13–20 on page 63.

7 Make two ears using black wool roving, then add a bit of beige wool roving to the inside. Attach the ears to the head, as shown in steps 22–24 on page 68.

8 For the parent, make the lower jaw using beige wool roving and attach it to the face beneath the snout. Use black wool roving to make a nose on the tip of the snout.

9 For the cub, use beige wool roving to make the nose. Embroider the mouth using red embroidery floss.

10 Stab a bit of loosened white wool roving onto the head to create circles for the eyes. Next, roll bits of black wool roving into balls and stab into place at the center of the white circles.

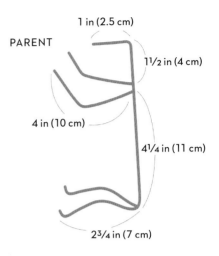

PARENT

1 in (2.5 cm)

1½ in (4 cm)

4 in (10 cm)

4¼ in (11 cm)

2¾ in (7 cm)

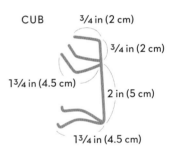

CUB

¾ in (2 cm)

¾ in (2 cm)

1¾ in (4.5 cm)

2 in (5 cm)

1¾ in (4.5 cm)

ELEPHANTS

SHOWN ON PAGE 28

MATERIALS

- Core fiber in white
- Wool roving
  A bit of gray
  A bit of pink
  A bit of dark pink
  A bit of black
  A bit of light blue
- 19-gauge aluminum wire
- Sport weight yarn in light brown

PROJECT DIAGRAM

CALF

Light blue

Base: Core fiber
Surface: Gray

Light
brown
yarn

Dark pink

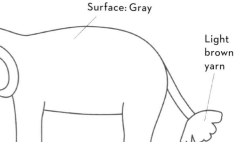

PARENT

Light blue

Base: Core fiber
Surface: Gray

Light
brown
yarn

Pink

Enlarge
200% for
full-size

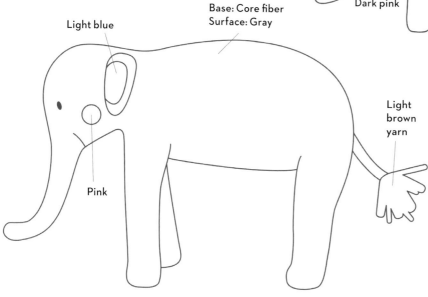

INSTRUCTIONS

1 Make the wire frame, as shown in steps 1–7 on page 67. Use the dimensions at right as a guide.

2 Wrap the yarn around the wire frame, as shown in step 8 on page 67.

3 Wrap the core fiber around the frame and stab in place, as shown in steps 3–5 on page 70.

4 Wrap gray wool roving around the base and stab to secure in place and shape the body, as shown in steps 6–7 on page 70.

5 Tie pieces of light brown yarn to the tail so they extend slightly beyond the wire. Next, wrap the tail with gray wool roving and stab in place.

6 Make two ears using gray wool roving, then add a bit of light blue wool roving to the inside. Attach the ears to the head, as shown in steps 22–24 on page 68.

7 Use black wool roving to make the eyes and mouth, as shown on page 38. Add a bit of loosened pink wool roving to the parent's cheeks or dark pink wool roving to the calf's cheeks.

PARENT

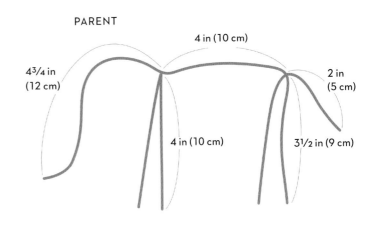

CALF

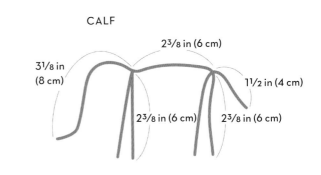

GIRAFFES

SHOWN ON PAGE 30

MATERIALS

- Core fiber in white
- Wool roving
  A bit of white
  A bit of rust
  A bit of orange
  A bit of light yellow
  A bit of dark brown
- 19-gauge aluminum wire
- Sport weight yarn in light brown

INSTRUCTIONS

1 Make the wire frame, as shown in steps 1–7 on page 67. Use the dimensions on page 127 as a guide.

2 Wrap the yarn around the wire frame, as shown in step 8 on page 67.

3 Wrap the core fiber around the frame and stab in place, as shown in steps 3–5 on page 70.

PROJECT DIAGRAM

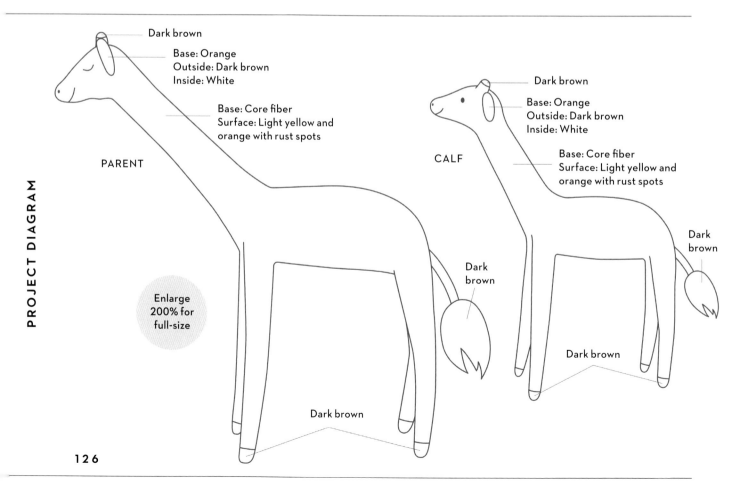

Dark brown

Base: Orange
Outside: Dark brown
Inside: White

Base: Core fiber
Surface: Light yellow and orange with rust spots

PARENT

Enlarge 200% for full-size

Dark brown

Dark brown

Base: Orange
Outside: Dark brown
Inside: White

Base: Core fiber
Surface: Light yellow and orange with rust spots

CALF

Dark brown

Dark brown

Dark brown

4. Make the hooves using dark brown wool roving, as shown in steps 14–16 on page 68. Make the legs thicker by wrapping with white wool roving and stabbing in place, as shown in step 17 on page 68. Add a bit of white wool roving to the nose.

5. Tie a tuft of dark brown wool roving to the tail so it extends slightly beyond the wire.

6. Cover the entire giraffe with a thin layer of light yellow wool roving. Leave the face and feet uncovered, as shown in the photo on page 30.

7. Add a thin layer of orange wool roving on top of the yellow. Refer to the photo on page 30 when adding orange wool roving around the face.

8. Make two ears using orange wool roving, then add a bit of white wool roving to the inside and dark brown wool roving to the outside. Attach the ears to the head, as shown in steps 22–24 on page 68.

9. Make two horns using orange wool roving. Attach to the head, then add a bit of dark brown wool roving to the tips.

10. Use small tufts of rust wool roving to make spots that cover the neck, body, and upper legs. Add a bit of rust wool roving to the back of the head.

11. Use dark brown wool roving to make a thin line for the mane, extending from the top of the head and down the neck.

12. Use dark brown wool roving to make the eyes, nostrils, and mouth, as shown on page 38.

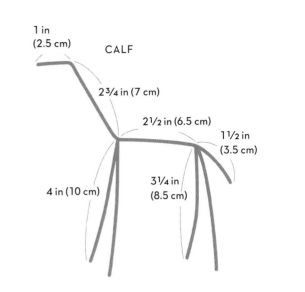

CALF

1 in (2.5 cm)
2¾ in (7 cm)
2½ in (6.5 cm)
1½ in (3.5 cm)
4 in (10 cm)
3¼ in (8.5 cm)

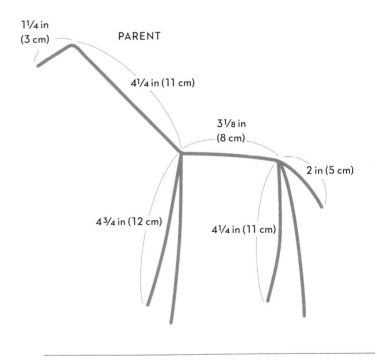

PARENT

1¼ in (3 cm)
4¼ in (11 cm)
3⅛ in (8 cm)
2 in (5 cm)
4¾ in (12 cm)
4¼ in (11 cm)

ABOUT THE AUTHOR

Makiko Arai is an animator and doll-maker living in Japan. After working for an animation production company for seven years, she began making dolls from wool felt and clay. In addition to writing books, Makiko holds workshops and designs kits and products. She is a member of the Japan Animation Association. Visit her website at araimakiko.com